A. T. Beng
J. O. Rose
Angola.
Ind.
W9-CCR-734

THE DIVINE CHALLENGE

THE DIVINE CHALLENGE

BY THE REV.

W. J. DAWSON, D. D.

HODDER & STOUGHTON
NEW YORK
GEORGE H. DORAN COMPANY

CONTENTS

THE DIVINE CHALLENGE

I

THE DIVINE CHALLENGE

"Believe Me that I am in the Father, and the Father in Me; or else believe Me for the very works' sake."—John xiv. 11.

DO men believe in Christ? Do the young men of this generation believe in Christ? If they do not, is it because they have paid no attention to the subject, and regard it as of slight importance? These are some of the questions suggested by this pregnant saying of Christ, to which I invite your deliberate and reverent attention.

Now beyond all doubt religion is by far the most important thing in human life. It is not merely a question of supreme interest who we are, what we are, and what is our destiny, but is a matter of supreme practical importance, since the whole area of human conduct is ruled by man's conception of himself, his duties, and his destiny. The evidence of this statement is found in universal history. Thus, for example, no state has ever risen to any position of great power and dominion except by the aid of religion, and the great struggles of mankind can almost always be traced to motives in themselves profoundly religious, or the offspring of religion. Perhaps the greatest empire the world has ever known was the Roman, and in the earlier stages of their history the Romans were not less religious than the Israelites. Horace was by no means a religious man, yet he was constrained to admit that Rome could not endure without religious convictions, and he warns his countrymen that all their sorrows spring from forgetfulness of God. Voltaire spoke in precisely the same spirit when he said that if there were no God it would be necessary to invent a God, because without belief in God the fabric of society could not be held together. So far as English domestic history is concerned, there has not been a single great struggle on English soil which has not been dominated by religious ideas, and the whole story of the national development expresses the enormous effect of religious ideas on practical conduct. So then the first thing which we are constrained to admit is the enormous importance of religion in personal and national life, and this is something which only the grossly ignorant or entirely foolish and thoughtless will think of doubting.

It was one of the earliest sayings of Jesus Christ that the practical virtue of any system of faith lay in its effect on conduct, "by their fruits ye shall know them." It is this principle which He applies now to Himself and His teaching. He submits Himself to the examination of practical men. He is well aware that in the long run even the best and greatest of men must be judged not by anything they have said or taught, but by what they have done. We all admit this principle and we practise it. When we sum up the career of a statesman, we may read his speeches with interest, but the main thing to which we pay attention is the nature of the measures he passed, and the total quality of his impact on the public life. When we read Buddha's teachings of brotherhood, we admit their charm, but we judge their real value by the fact that for four thousand years in India the lives of the rich and the poor have run in parallel lines, and have never once met. A man's ideas and teachings are at all times but the flower of the mind, or of the soul, if you will; the great question is, is there fruit as well as flower, and has the blossom slowly changed into the fruit that is for the healing of the nations? Jesus knows that that question must be asked, and He not merely submits to it, He challenges it. Standing in the sad gloom of the premature end, knowing that His disciples will be tempted to think His life a failure, He now bids them, if they cannot believe in Him for His own sake, at least to believe in Him for His works' sake. Let them measure that work; let them regard the significance of Christ in history; and then let them judge whether or not He is divine. And that is the challenge of Christ to us also. We see what

His disciples did not see, we behold the expanding and miraculous phenomenon of Christianity through nearly twenty centuries — the significance of Christ in history, the supremacy that He has won over the souls and minds of men, the effect which belief in Him has had over all who have truly embraced it, and through them, over great tracts of time, wide fields of event, immense domains of thought, morals and conduct — we see this, and ask, "Could a mere man do this?" Was not this the very God incarnate, God made manifest in Jesus, so that He who has wrought these wonders in the world might truly claim, "I am in the Father, and the Father in me; I and the Father are one."

For the sake of clearness in definition we may say, that the works of Christ are manifest in three directions — the mind, the heart, and the conduct of men. His work upon the mind is seen in the intellectual ideals of men; on the heart, in their moral life; on the conduct, in their practical life. Let us put aside if you will, all questions of the person of Christ. Let us assume that all which we know is that many centuries ago there appeared in an obscure village of the obscurest country in the world, a young man, who for three years aroused considerable interest among His countrymen. By all accounts He had the genius to be loved, and to be hated; He made friends and He made enemies; He disregarded the prejudices and conventions of society; He taught certain rules of life that were new and strange; He fell at last a victim to a jealous ecclesiastic oligarchy, was violently arrested, unjustly condemned, crucified, dead, and buried. His teachings survived Him, and by-and-bye the story of His life, as was perfectly natural, came to be told. These teachings, first impregnating the minds of a few humble men, spread with an unprecedented rapidity, and had the most singular and momentous effect upon the world. That is as much as we need to know for the purpose of our argument; the question is what were those effects, and how do they dispose our minds to think of Christ?

First, then, I ask you to think of the work of Christ in the realm of the intellect; and let us further narrow the enquiry to the consideration of the religious ideas with which He impregnated the human mind.

Now if we go back to the date of Christ's birth, we find preserved for us by the diligence of the historian a vivid and accurate picture of the religious condition of the world. Three nations at once absorb our attention, the Jew, the Greek, and the Roman. All that was wisest in human philosophy and profoundest in human thought was preserved among these three peoples. It was to these peoples that Christianity especially addressed itself. It was in Jerusalem, Corinth, Ephesus, and Rome that the earliest seed of Christianity was sown. What then was the religious condition of these great peoples, what the conclusions of the intellect on religious subjects which they had reached and accepted?

The answer may be given in a single sentence; in each case religion had totally broken down.

For the Jew religion had become narrower and narrower until it was a mere piece of gorgeous and empty ritual. Its theory of the divine government of the universe had become incredible. Amid the millions of men and women in the world who vaguely felt after the secret of virtue, it would appear that God cared only for the Jew. To be a son of Abraham was to have an inalienable claim on heaven, and, according to the Pharisee's view of the case, quite apart from any righteousness of conduct. God was thus merely a tribal God, and the whole universe was administered in the special interest of the Jew. A great religion when it was enunciated on Sinai, a powerful religion when it gripped the mind and conscience of a fugitive race in their early struggles, a true religion when it was sincerely believed; it had now lost all its saving salt of sincerity, had become a fetish, and ministered less to human virtue than to human impiety, arrogance, and exclusiveness.

Among the Greeks also religion had totally broken down. The worship of mere physical beauty was universal, and when Socrates prayed that the Gods would give him "beauty of soul," he was not understood. The Gods themselves were the incarnation of human vices as well as virtues, for the Greek had his God of cunning, and his God of lying, as well as his Gods of music, chastity, and wisdom.

And among the Romans the breakdown of religion was even more disastrous, and it took a form absolutely appalling. That form was the worship of Cæsar as God. When Herod received the worship of the people as a God and not as a man; when Paul spoke of the "man of sin who sitteth in the temple of God shewing himself that he is God," Herod simply emulated the Cæsars in claiming divine honours, and Paul directly refers to this impious worship of Cæsar. To the reigning Cæsar, temples were built, sacrifices were offered, and divine honours were paid. To us such an impiety seems incredible, especially among a people so robust in mind and masculine in temper as the Roman. But there was a reason for it. Faith in any external government of the universe had wholly failed. Madness and corruption had seized upon every class of society. There was neither justice, virtue, nor morality left — all had been dissolved with a dissolving faith in a divine government. Then came Julius Cæsar, and, by what is the greatest miracle of secular history, arrested the decay of society, imposed upon it a military despotism which was at least just and powerful, combined its scattered forces, gave Rome a new lease of life, and established once more the supremacy of virtue. What wonder that Cæsar was soon regarded as more than mortal man? What wonder that the hope of mankind clung with frantic, and then with adoring passion to this new Saviour of society? Something man must worship, and the Gods being gone, soon man began to worship his fellow man as God. And this was the state of religious thought when Christ came — the Jew worshipping before an empty shrine on which the flame of sincerity had died, the Greek delighting in a brutally corrupt mythology, the Roman worshipping Augustus Cæsar as the one puissant and active deity in the world.

And now consider the challenge of this text. This youth, growing up in a tiny Syrian town, where not only the Roman or the Greek but the leaders of His own nation never came, begins to speak certain words about God. The only conception of God left to the Jews is an exclusive tribal deity who cares only for the sons of Abraham; this youth speaks of the Father in heaven, who has an equal love of all men. The Greek looking with impure eyes into the mystery of things invents deities even more corrupt than man; this youth says, "Blessed are the pure in heart for they shall see God." The Roman, bankrupt in all faith in any divine power outside the earth, sacrifices to Cæsar as the only power he knows; this youth draws back the veil of the infinite, and reveals the ever-living Judge of quick and dead, and says, "There is none good but one, that is God." You would have supposed that any words spoken by one so insignificant would have been wholly lost; it is natural to suppose so. What is there briefer in its influence than the spoken word; and this youth never wrote a single sentence, never did what the humblest prophet or philosopher did to perpetuate His message, never took the least precaution to preserve His teaching. Yet that teaching spread with miraculous rapidity. He Himself had said that His words were spirit and life, and so it proved. Whispered at first in the lowly places of the earth, spoken presently in the market places, temples and palaces; prescribed as heresy, hated as blasphemy; these words spread and everywhere they struck the note of a new life. Into the deep blackness of the pit where society lay and rotted there came a ray of light; over the sterile waste of human thought there blew the wind of life. At length the hour came when the old was utterly outworn; Rome fell, and great was the fall of it; but in the same instant it was discovered that a new power had taken its place, and Christ filled the throne which Cæsar had abdicated. The dust of conflict cleared away, and behold the Cross shone upon the Capitol. The thoughts of Christ about God became the supreme truths on which men based all their hopes and aspirations. The Fatherhood of God — a true sovereignty of intelligence, law, and love — became the keystone of human thought, and a new world sprang out of the ruins of the old. All that as the fruit of a brief life lived in Galilee, and of certain words spoken among its quiet hills; all that as the work of one who had but three years in which to influence the world, and was rejected by the world with every circumstance of ignominy and shame! Have you considered what it means? Have you given one single thoughtful hour to what is the greatest phenomenon in human history? Can you, with this phenomenon before you, resist the force of the divine appeal, "Believe me, that I am in the Father, and the Father in me; or else believe me for the very works' sake?"

Let a second picture pass before the mind, and consider the work of Christ upon the human heart. The heart stands for morality; for the way in which men feel toward one another, and the way in which they treat one another.

And here three facts may be stated as indicative of the moral condition of the world when Christ entered it. The first is that the ancient world had no conception of the rights of human liberty. The great mass of men in the Roman empire were slaves, and when Plato sketched his ideal republic, it never occurred to him that society could exist without slavery. The great edifices of the ancient world which yet remain, on whose spoliated splendour we look with wonder, were all built by slave labour.

There is no truism in modern philosophy more worn and trite than the dignity of labour, the "perennial nobleness of honest toil," as Carlyle called it; we sometimes forget that this is an ethic of very modern date. Labour for the Roman was a thing both contemptible and shameful. Society had but two classes, the free citizen and the slave. An immense gulf separated them; on one side of the gulf, life moved in stateliness and ease, a sensual and sumptuous pageant; on the other, life toiled obscurely in ignorance and drudgery, knowing no rights, and incapable of striving for them. So again, the ancient world knew nothing of morality in our sense of the term. One of the chief Pauline doctrines is that society is an organism; that it is knit together by a thousand delicate nerves; that our good actions and our bad involve others in our weal and woe, and that there is no man who liveth to himself. But to the wisest of Pagan philosophers such words meant nothing. Seneca, one of the clearest of ancient thinkers, made no scruple of advising Nero to give the rein to his passions, and it never occurred to the philosopher that the pleasures of Nero involved the misery and dishonour of his victims. That would be our first thought in considering any question of morality, but it was a thought of which the ancient world had never heard.

It does not surprise us therefore to find further that the ancient world knew no pity for weakness or misfortune. The reign of might, and the right of might were things unquestioned. If a man chose to torture his slave or even slay his child, it was his own affair. To be weak or poor, was not only to be miserable, but deservedly miserable. Life had little value, and of the eighty thousand people who filled the Colosseum, and watched the dying gladiator, "butchered to make a Roman holiday," not one ever thought of pitying him. Nor was even the Jew much better than the Roman in his attitude to misfortune and weakness. The blind man doubtless deserved his blindness, or he would not be blind; suffering was the wrath of heaven; and the one convincing proof of the favour of God was a visible prosperity; and thus, put in a slightly different way, for the Jew also, as for the Roman, might was the only right.

Once more look then at this supreme phenomenon of history, the work of Christ upon the human heart. This youth comes down from the hill-village of Nazareth, moves among all classes of society, and treats them as having equal rights. He announces the golden axiom that as we would that men shall do to us, even so should we do to them, and He practises it. He goes about doing good, healing, comforting, feeding the hungry, visiting the sick, succouring the dying pariahs and wastrels of society; He earns the splendid reproach that He is the friend of publicans and sinners. He utters parable after parable, the aim of which is to teach kindliness and love; applauds the good Samaritan; rebukes Dives, pities Lazarus; pictures the Judgment-seat of God as the solemn tribunal where men are judged for their love of one another, or their lovelessness; Himself dies forgiving His enemies, and breathing benediction on a thief who perishes with Him. At the time, perhaps, not even His disciples comprehended the significance of these words and actions; but they were not forgotten. After a while they emerged into dazzling distinctness, and attracted the attention of the world. Men meditated over them, talked of them one to another, and at last strove to live in the same spirit. A company of men and women arose whose avowed object was to live as this youth lived, and they began to overspread the world. And so the Church of Christ begins — a confederacy of men and women who love Him, love one another, and love all men; the religion of humanity begins; pity, tenderness, and consideration soften the human heart; slavery dies out, gladiatorial combats cease; wealth is shared, poverty is cheerfully endured, labour becomes honourable, and the keynote of a new morality is struck, that it is more blessed to give than to receive — to minister than to be ministered unto. All this as the fruit of a single brief life lived long ago in Palestine. All our liberties, rights, humanities, moralities as the direct result of a life that perished on the Cross! How will you judge that life? What can you make of a story so splendid and so nearly incredible? Forget if you please all that theology has to say about this wondrous youth of Nazareth; regard it as unthinkable if you must; still the works remain, and the divine challenge reaches us, " Believe me that I am in the Father, and the Father in me: or else believe me for the very works' sake."

And so you have the last picture of the work of Christ on the practical conduct of men — and here we have no need to confine our thoughts to the ancient world, for the work of Christ is seen all around us in the characteristics of our own time.

Far away yonder in the Southern seas lies a country that we call Fiji. Sixty years ago it was barbarous and cannibal. To that dark land of blood and the shadow of death Christian Missionaries went. They toiled, they suffered, they died, and some of them were murdered. Others took their places, and these also in their turn suffered and died. They were men of no genius, but they had a story to tell, and they told it. They spoke unceasingly of Christ, of His love, His pity, and His death; and they themselves lived as those with whom love was the master-word of life. To-day Fiji is Christian. Cannibalism is no more, virtue and truth are loved, brotherhood reigns, and the lips that once drank the blood of the slain, drink the cup of the Communion of Christ the Lord.

You need not go back to the days of the Roman empire to discover what Christ has done for humanity; nothing in the past is more wonderful than this present-day story of Fiji; and Christ says, "If ye believe me not for my words' sake, believe me for Fiji's sake."

In the history of the world from time to time men arise who exercise a vast redemptive influence upon their times — the Wesleys, the Moffats, the Livingstones. They discard wealth, reject ease, scorn fame; they are found preaching to the brutal mobs who stone them, living among the lowest of the race, loving them, and dying for them. They have left us in no doubt as to the secret of their lives; they tell us that the love of Christ constrained them. Christ may be to you a dim historic figure, but He was not so to them; to them He was a real and living Master, whose presence they felt, whose word they obeyed, whose spirit was reincarnated in them; and from their lives the challenge rings, "If ye believe not my words, and find in my Gospel nothing that moves or interests you, then believe me for Wesley's sake, for Moffat's sake, for Livingstone's sake."

Round about us rise a series of institutions of which the world in former times never so much as dreamed. We have our hospitals, our orphanages, our asylums for every species of human misery. We have a vast array of public buildings called churches, and there is not one of them which is not a centre of philanthropic effort to befriend the weak, to help the poor, to succour the sorrowful. There is not a hospital in the land that was not built by the hands of this youth of Nazareth. There is not an asylum for indigence and misery that does not owe itself to Calvary. Abolish Christianity, and in a single generation all would be swept away, for it is by the munificence of Christians, and them alone, that such hospices of mercy exist. We may find the theology of the Churches hard to be understood, and we may have no taste for the casuistries of the theologians; Christ bids us turn from them if we must, and addresses us in other words: "If ye believe not Me for my words' sake, believe me for the sake of the hospital and the orphanage, for the sake of the pity men have learned of Me, and of the love which I have taught them."

It is a common error to treat Christianity as if it were a disputable philosophy; it is not a philosophy, it is a practical fact, and a vital force. Do not think that you have done with Christianity when you have found some glaring fault in its professors, or some illogical passage in the statements of its advocates. Christianity is the greatest phenomenon in history, and its proof is its works. If you have paid no attention to that phenomenon it is no credit to your intelligence. You give eager attention enough to a thousand other things that are of the very slightest importance, to the pleasures of life, to what is called success in life, to the theories of this or that popular teacher, to political or social programmes that will be forgotten in a year — to sport, to amusement, to athletics, to the ephemeral trivialities of a passing literature — but what think ye of Christ? Have you ever considered that question? Have you ever given one single hour of earnest and continuous thought to the phenomenon of Jesus? Have you ever realised that all you have and are is bound up in that question? Have you ever realised, in a word, that the question of religion is the one supreme question, and that until man has found the answer to it he disquiets himself in vain, and walketh in a vain show? That is the conclusion I would press home upon you. Go home, and face the question, "What do I think of Christ, what has Christ done for me, what claim has He upon me?" Go out into the world of business to-morrow and remember that it is Christ's world you live in, and that you are not your own, you are bought with a price. Go from this church, and in the quiet of your own heart, clear and insistent above all other questions that agitate you, hear this divine, this cogent, this pathetic challenge, "*Believe me that I am in the Father, and the Father in Me; or else Believe Me for the very works' sake.*"

THE LAMP AND THE DAY STAR

II

THE LAMP AND THE DAY STAR

"And we have the word of prophecy made more sure; whereunto ye do well to take heed, as unto a lamp shining in a dark place, until the day dawn, and the day star arise in your heart."—2 Peter i. 19.

NOTHING is more striking from the point of view of psychology than the enormous effect which Jesus had on the minds of His immediate followers. Even were we disposed to doubt the truth of the historic resurrection of Jesus, we should find it impossible to deny that He rose again in a very real sense in the lives of His apostles. The thoughts they think are His thoughts: the hopes and emotions they feel are His hopes and emotions: and we know that these thoughts, hopes and emotions are totally different from those they once cherished, and are even diametrically opposed to them. When St. Paul says, "I live yet not I but Christ liveth in me," he proclaims this phenomenon — a phenomenon so startling and profound that it stands alone in the history of the human mind. Moreover, St. Paul is at pains to tell us that for a considerable period of his life Jesus was nothing to him, and that there was not a thought in his heart that was not opposed to Him. And what was true of Paul was true of all the apostles. They each represent a new incarnation of Jesus. In each the soul of Jesus has been re-born: born again in the heart by faith, is the apostle's phrase. Thus we find the whole mind of Peter penetrated with the sense of Jesus. The Galilean fisherman is extinct; Jesus lives in him the hope of glory. One sublime image is in all his thoughts, colours all his writings, pervades all his emotions — and that is the image of his Lord. Past, present, and future are all focussed in Jesus, and so in this passage when he surveys the history of things past and the course of things to come, he perceives all alike in the light of Him who is the Alpha and Omega, the beginning and the end, and the bright and morning star of Hope and Truth.

Notice the imagery of this passage. It is very beautiful and poetic — a series of pictures full of significance and charm. You have first a picture of the world and of the human heart, as a dark place: literally a squalid place, and by this term the Greek meant a place without light and without water. It is a region of pain and dissatisfaction: a wilderness, a barbarous place, a land of darkness and the shadow of death. But it is not wholly dark: even in this land of gloom men move with lamps, searching for a practicable way that is firm and safe. These men are the prophets, the guides, and shepherds of humanity. The lamp they carry is a light unto the feet — light sufficient for the next step of duty, but it casts no extended ray, and paints the curtain of impenetrable darkness with a glimmering splendour only. Yet it is much to have any light in a pitch-black night, and these light-bearers lead the host of humanity on many a crooked path, as a peasant with a lamp may guide the traveller through the defiles of a mountain range. Perhaps the very image in the mind of Peter is a scene often witnessed by him in the old Galilean days — the shepherd on the hills whose lamp burns all night beside the sleeping flocks; a lamp of hope in the dark waste and emptiness of night.

But now he sees another thing also; the dawn begins to break. The shepherd's lamp burns dim, fades to a tiny spark, and is extinguished in the widening light. Over the wide glimmering hills a star hangs, and the heavens grow lucid round it, for it is the morning star. The clouds melt into a veil of gossamer: one by one the lamps are put out, for the long vigil is over, and the day is here. Even so, says Peter, God gave the lamps of prophecy in the world's great night. Through long ages the prophets, those lonely lamp-bearers, lighting the world's advance, did their duty: until at last the morning star of Christ appeared, the day of God broke over Bethlehem and Calvary, and the light of the world had come.

The Lamp and the Day Star.— Let us take another illustration, which lies perhaps within the experience of some of you. Suppose we were setting out to climb some lonely Alpine peak, what would be the method of our advance? The first part of the journey would begin soon after midnight. Those who watched us as we went would see a string of lights moving up the mountain side, and by these glimmering human stars we should find our way through the thick pine forest, up the steep moraine, across the glacier. Above us there would rise a dome of sky dark as velvet, and far away the white ice peaks would stand like ghostly sentinels, each hooded in his snows, silent, dreadful, immutable. But at three or four o'clock, as we gained some wide plateau of snow, a halt would be called. Through the silent air a sigh of life would rise: far away the topmost peak would grow whiter; round us the outlines of ice and rock would emerge into distinctness, and then the guides would extinguish the lamps one by one. Why? Because their use was ended: the summer dawn is near, and already on the peaks the rose of day begins to burn. This is precisely the contrast which is suggested in this poetic phrase of Peter's. Lamps and the morning star — lamps and the sun: for the people that sat in darkness have seen a great light. Uncertainty is exchanged for certainty: the perilous path, half-discerned, for the safe and practicable way: the guesses of Philosophy for the perfect day of Truth. The day is come, for Christ has come: put out thy lamp, O shepherd of the hills, and thou, also, solitary climber after truth, for the day star arises in thine heart, and

> Out of the shadow of night
> The world rolls into light,
> It is daybreak everywhere.

The Lamp and the Day Star — each may stand as a symbol of hope — the contrast suggested is a contrast of degree. Human hopes take two forms: the individual and the collective. Something in the human heart makes man hope for himself — bids him know he was not made to die, bids him seek a brighter destiny than that which seems included in, or indicated by, his earthly lot. And from that personal hope he passes naturally to that collective hope which is the spirit of human progress. Unlike every other creature of this earth, man does not take his lot as he finds it. He is continually seeking to modify and improve it. He is always experimenting in the art of living. To-day he is a tent-dweller, to-morrow the builder of cities. He interrogates earth and air, sea and sky, for their secrets: finds them, uses them and shapes them to his own demands. He invents schemes of government, codes of law, maxims of conduct. Century by century he debates about these things, clears and sifts his thoughts, and extends their range. And in all this he is inspired by a belief in Society; he sees it as an organism that grows, and may be helped in its growth, until at last something perfect shall be found, and the desert shall bloom and blossom as the rose. So man has thought and acted from the beginning, because as each man enters the world an angel puts into his hand a lamp, sets him on an upward path, and bids him hope.

Turn then to the times before Christ, and ask, what about these hopes? What had they done for man, and to what point had he attained? The highest individual hope is found in the Hebrew Scriptures. Were all revealed religion finally proclaimed incredible, we should still owe a debt to the Jew which is incalculable. For the Jew, taught by his own political experience that from a minute and despised germ of life a great nation might be evolved; taught by his own spiritual experience that virtue and righteousness are the sole abiding realities; taught by his own intellectual experience that truth might be won and kept, and become the living soul of nations — the Jew has accomplished this imperishable, this immeasurable service to humanity — he has bid it hope. Into the darkness and mystery of the world he has penetrated with a bolder step than all his fellows, and he has borne aloft a brighter lamp. But when we begin to measure the circumference of splendour cast by that lamp, we perceive at once that it did not go very far. On some problems where light was most desired, it shed but a feeble and fluctuating ray.

Thus for example the Hebrew Scriptures as a whole say little of personal immortality. If you turn to the words of Hezekiah — one of the wisest and most pious of Jewish kings, when he is suddenly brought face to face with the unknown beyond death — you will find that that unknown holds nothing for him. He clings vehemently to life and gives his reason thus: "The grave cannot praise Thee, death cannot celebrate Thee: they that go down into the pit cannot hope for thy truth." The words of Job, in spite of occasional and brief harp-notes of triumph, ring with the same accent of entire mournfulness: death is for him the place of darkness, the house of dust where the very stones are darkness, and of which the best that can be said is that there the wicked cease from troubling and the weary are at rest. There is little to choose between such passages as these and that great Assyrian hymn of death, called the Descent of Istar into Hades, which pictures the abode of the dead as

The house of darkness
The house men enter but cannot depart from,
The road men go but cannot return,
The house from whose dwellers the light is withdrawn
The place where dust is their food, their nourishment
clay.
The light they behold not: in darkness they dwell,
They are clothed like birds, all fluttering wings,
On the door and the gate posts the dust lies thick,

And so without turning to many a passage in the Psalms and to the dreary words of Solomon, with their unutterable despair, we see that the hopefulness of the Hebrew was far more circumscribed than we supposed. It was a lamp, not the day star, not the day; it lit the path of earthly duty with a perfect light, but it cast barely a ray into the impenetrable darkness of the shadow of death and that which lay beyond it.

The same thing may be said, though with some modification, about the social hopes of the Hebrew. The lamp burned bright and unextinguished for many an age, for of all things the surest thing to the Jew was that it is righteousness which ennobles a nation. He saw the vision of a perfect society — a society God-governed, God-worshipping — the perfect vehicle of the divine will, the concrete expression of the divine mind. But what he also found to be true at every point of his history was that he was not efficient to create and maintain such a society. He was like the artist who has the genius to prepare the scheme of a great picture, but has not the power to complete it. Thus we have only to turn to our Gospels to discover that Jewish society as Christ found it was hollow to the core. It was, as He said, in an image at once startling and dreadful, a whited sepulchre, full of dead men's bones and all uncleanness. Religious and moral progress had come to a standstill. The priesthood was powerful and imposing but corrupt: the leaders of the nation learned in the pedantry of learning, but insincere in belief, immoral in conduct, and hypocrites in temper and practice. The lamp had shown the way, but had not led men to the height: and as the ages passed it had ever burned dimmer, till the way itself grew indistinct. It was a lamp whose light was dying in the socket — not a day star, not the pure unvanquishable dawn; the light of a lamp upon the vast interminable ice-slopes of human duty.

And if we pass beyond the Jew to that great Pagan world which surrounded him, we find things immeasurably worse. Both the Greek and the Roman had given up hope of any spiritual destiny beyond death. As for society it had reached its climax — it stood still. Here and there a philosopher still talked nobly of his ideal republic, as Plato did; but none listened, and none cared to listen. For, of this great Pagan world, ruled by the splendid but monotonous Roman order, it was emphatically true that the whole scheme of society seemed fixed and immutable. If change came at all it would be change for the worse: and indeed already much had changed for the worse, for the old simple religious beliefs, the primitive manliness and virtue of the Roman were as stars extinguished in the gathering night of a general depravity. If men looked forward it was not with hope; it was to cry

> Here is the moral of all human tales,
> 'Tis but the same rehearsal of the past,
> First freedom and then glory; when that fails,
> Wealth, vice, corruption — barbarism at last.

So far the lamps of human wisdom had led men, but no further, and the place in which it now shone was a dark place indeed, for hope scarcely illumined it at all, and in it the waters of peace and life were not found.

And now listen to the sublime and inspired speech of Peter: *a lamp shining in a dark place, until the day dawn, and the day star arise in your hearts.* Do not the words lead us back at once to those green pastures where shepherds watched their flocks by night and suddenly heard a great company of the heavenly host proclaiming peace and good will to man? Is he not thinking of the Star which arose in the East, and stood still over the manger-cradle where the young child lay? Are not these shepherds, and these wise men whose lamps hang extinguished because the glory of the Lord shone around them, types of the world's sages and prophets whose lamps of wisdom paled their ineffectual ray, because at last the day star rises, and the morning breaks? For this and no other was precisely what did happen with the coming of Christ. He came as the Light of the world, bringing with Him all the fresh hope and splendour of the morning. For man the individual, immeasurable hope — the shadow of death gone, and life and immortality brought to light by the Gospel. For man collectively, that is for society, immeasurable hope also: the old order changed and giving place to new, and the spirit of progress once more passing over the dark void, and quickening it. Man rises up and sees the peaks of God afar, the immortal summits long hidden in the night, or visible only like vague shadows in the gloom, and presses on to a destiny such as eye hath not seen, nor ear heard, nor the heart of man conceived. Society long stagnant, fixed and immutable, begins to move also, and the spirit of progress is abroad. The Roman order gives place to a diviner order, the empire of the Cæsars to the Kingdom of God, the religion of force and terror to the religion of humanity. It was not only Christ who was born in Bethlehem — the world itself was born anew there. All history ranks itself, not by the caprice of the ecclesiastic, but by force of natural affinity, into that which came before Christ, and that which happened after. The most sceptical of historians must needs admit the classification: whatever happened in Bethlehem, this he knows, that a force was born there that transformed the world. That force was the Birth of Light; the lamps that lit the night are gone, the prophets' toil and the shepherds' vigil are fulfilled. The Day star has risen, and behind it comes the Day streaming into the dark heart of man, illumining the way of Truth, glittering on the far off pinnacles of the city of God, filling even the pathways of the tomb with an immortal sunshine — the Day has come, for Christ has come.

Lamps and the Morning Star.— Such a contrast further teaches us how we should regard the ancient religions of the world. There was a time not far removed when Christian men refused to hear a good word for any other religion than Christianity because they imagined that it was necessary to minify and even defame every other system of religious thought in order to magnify Christianity. That was not the spirit of Christ: He came not to destroy but to fulfil all the broken hints of truth and goodness in all the long course of human thought and conduct. These ancient religions were the lamps lit by the human soul in a dark place. Light is always light, and the feeblest light is really lit at the sun, which is the source of all light. And a spark of the true light shone in the soul of Confucius when five hundred years before Christ, he formulated his golden rule, "What you do not wish done to yourself, do not do to others." It shone in Zoroaster, it shone in Socrates, it shone conspicuously in Buddha. All honour to the lamp bearers of humanity, by whatever name they were called. All honour to the men of spiritual genius, who in every age held aloft the torch of truth, and, dying, passed it on, so that the world should not stumble and wholly fall in the dense gloom of ignorance and folly. But they were lamp bearers only. They illumined one little section of human thought — one brief step upon the way; when the Day comes all is illumined. And as the day literally fulfils the broken gleams of starry fire that pierced the night, so Christ fulfils all that Confucius and Buddha taught, all that Socrates and Zoroaster hoped. The lamp is quenched because the morning grows. And when we take Christ to the great nations of the East, it is not in a spirit of contempt for the only religion they know; it is rather with thankfulness to God that they have any religion, and that God hath not left Himself without a witness in their hearts; and when we preach Christ under the shadow of Chinese pagodas and Indian temples, it is only that we may change the lamps of Confucius and Buddha for the brightness of the morning star; for Christ is the desire of all nations, and these great creators of religious thought in a hundred nations kept vigil till He appeared, were His unconscious light bearers, and were as those who watched for the coming of the morning, even of the perfect day of Him who is the Light of life.

Lamps and the Morning Star.— Perhaps some of you will say, But after all is not this exquisite story of the birth of Jesus mere legend; may it not also be pure myth? Let us concede that it is both myth and legend if you will, as Mr. Grant Allen contends in his latest and most serious contribution to literature, but even then, there are two indisputable and obstinate truths to be resolved; one is that something happened, and that that something changed the world; the other is that mere myths do not change the world. It is this very accusation of the mythical character of Christianity which Peter answers in his Epistle, when he says he has not followed cunningly devised fables, for he was an eye witness of the majesty of Christ and had had every opportunity which the most incredulous could desire of learning the truth at the fountain head. And again, he himself, a changed man, moving among changed men, with a Christian church growing up around him which is already beginning to profoundly influence the Roman empire, is a witness that something happened and is happening. Jesus for him was no myth, he had sat with Him at the last supper, he had seen Him die upon the cross. His birth was no legend; he had known those who had watched His childhood, and had pondered in their hearts the story of Bethlehem. It was not a myth which was finding its way into every corner of the empire and had its converts in Cæsar's household also; it was rather the light of a great reality, a supreme revelation. He stood amid the dying lamps of the ancient world, as one may stand in a great city when the night departs, and he saw the Day grow round him. He could not be mistaken: and if he could, we cannot; for from the moment that the star rested over Bethlehem, the whole world has grown brighter. And to that world that was, that dark hard world where

> Weariness and sated lust
> Made human life a hell,

— that midnight world, with its faint and scattered lamps of truth, we are not likely to go back, even upon the invitation of Mr. Grant Allen. We have seen the Day: let those prefer the night who will. We have exchanged the lamp for the morning star — we are not likely to repent our choice. Light of Hope and Light of Truth, still grow brighter, is our cry: Thy Kingdom come: and to those who see it not, those who are blind amid the blaze of noon, those who still grope at the altars of a dead paganism, and stumble on the tombs of a long-buried philosophy, we can but utter the great apostolic appeal, "Awake, thou that sleepest, and arise from the dead, and Christ shall give thee light."

And so the words of Peter take us back to Bethlehem. Dark lies the Jewish plain, dark rise the Syrian hills, hushed lie the pastures and the sheep; and on these hills, invisible, stand men of majestic presence, the great spirits of the past — Moses, Samuel, David, Isaiah, and that Elijah who was a burning and a shining light — they stand and wait. "Watchman what of the night?" But no voice answers from the sleeping pastures, and the world lies dumb. "Watchman what of the night? Our lamps go out, and something tells us that our long vigil is nearly done." But none replies: the heavens are very still, and up the road to the little town of Bethlehem, climb two weary pilgrims for whom there is no room in the inn. "Watchman what of the night?" And now behold the fugitives have reached their humble shelter, and a child's voice floats out upon the frosty air, and a whisper runs across the world—"The night is departing." Lonely watchers, majestic prophets of the truth, depart ye also to your rest—the world is safe, for God hath entered it. He enters it in the garb of a little child. He enters it—and light enters with Him: for suddenly a great glory floods the earth, and a multitude of the heavenly host sing

> Glory to God in the highest
> And on earth peace, good will among men.

So is Christ born in Bethlehem of Judea, and from land to land there flies the news, "The night is gone, the long expected Day has come."

THE SOVEREIGNTY OF GOD

III

THE SOVEREIGNTY OF GOD

"When He giveth quietness who then can make trouble, and when He hideth His face who then can behold Him?"—Job. xxxiv. 29.

THE Book of Job deals in dramatic form with the most solemn of all problems, the Mystery of Human suffering. It is the greatest dramatic poem in the world, and in all the centuries which have elapsed since its production, human thought never soared higher, nor plumbed deeper into the mystery of things. It does not pretend wholly to solve the problem of suffering, but it advances five theories,[1] each one of which is eagerly debated, and all of which are finally swallowed up in the glory of the Divine intervention. The first theory is that suffering is the test of saintship, and that by the endurance of suffering, human nature arrives at saintship — a theory which Job himself favours, when he finally says, "He knoweth the way that I take; when He hath tried me, I shall come forth as gold." The second theory is: that all suffering is

[1] The analysis is borrowed from Professor Moulton's masterly introduction on the Book of Job.

in some way a judgment upon sin, a theory which Job indignantly repudiates, because he is unable to accuse himself of any wrong-doing, which could justly merit punishment so monstrous. A third theory is that suffering is sent to call men to repentance, and is thus a mercy since by repentance man may avert total destruction — a theory to which Job shows himself entirely indifferent. A fourth theory is that the whole universe is full of mystery, and the mystery of evil is not greater than the mystery of good — a theory hinted at in this passage of the drama, "God hides His face, who then can behold Him": *i. e.*, who can pretend to read the reasons why God performs any act whatever? A fifth theory is that the right attitude toward mystery is entire faith, and that mystery is thus necessary to the growth of faith, and is as the dews of Eden that keep the garden of the soul fresh — a theory which finds ample illustration in the way in which Job endures his trial. Thus the thoughts of men circle round the problem of suffering, and the ages have not changed these thoughts. Job is still afflicted in a thousand homes: Job's comforters still appear in a thousand schemes of philosophy and religion: and the endless drama still enacts itself on a stage where mournful trumpets blow, and tears fall, and the sombre pageant of sorrow unfolds itself before those who are the witnesses of pain to-day, and may be its victims to-morrow.

But you will observe that toward one point all these conflicting theories converge, and that is the truth of the absolute sovereignty of God. The one thing that is doubted by no one in the drama, is that God reigns. The Potter may or may not act unjustly by His clay, but none can deny His right. If it be God's will to afflict Job, who shall say Him nay? This is of course one of the oldest, as it is one of the saddest, thoughts in the world. You catch its echo in some of the more despairing utterances of the Hebrew prophets, and particularly in Jeremiah's great parable of the Potter and the Wheel. You have it distinctly stated in the poetry of the Persian Omar, who flourished in the first quarter of our Twelfth century — when he cries that we are all

> But helpless Pieces of the game He plays,
> Upon this chequer-board of nights and days:
> Hither and thither moves, and checks and slays,
> And one by one back in the closet lays.

You have it stated afresh with infinite bitterness in the concluding words of Hardy's "Tess"— "Justice was done: and the President of the Immortals had ended His sport with Tess." And Hardy himself in using the phrase sends us back to the old Greek dramatists, all of whom felt a terror of the Gods, and felt themselves impotent before their wrath and their injustice. The absolute sovereignty of God, the indeterminable power of the Creator over

His creatures, His perfect right to do as He will with man, regardless either of the merit or demerit of the individual — this is, as I have said, one of the oldest as it is one of the saddest thoughts of the world, and has filled the human heart with terror and misgiving.

But you will observe at once that this thought is very far from producing in Elihu either sadness or incurable despair. Elihu is the youngest of the speakers in the drama, and he speaks with all the confidence of youth, with all its optimism, with all its sense of having obtained a new knowledge denied to the elders. How far his wisdom surpassed theirs it is not for us now to discuss, but it will be seen at once that he uses this tremendous truth of the absolute sovereignty of God in a new way, and draws from it not the lessons of despair but of hope. It affects him in two ways. He first states the absolute apportionment of good in men's lives —" When He giveth quietness, who then can make trouble? " Whatever we may or may not know of God, we do know that He gives good gifts to men — that He gives some good gift to every man, and from that we may argue that in the main His government of the world is not cruel or unjust. The second thing he states is the concealment of the Highest Good, which is the vision of God, the perfect knowledge of His ways — " When God hideth His face, who then can behold Him? " In all lives, and even in those which we may variously call the happiest or the most fortunate, there is something hidden, something withdrawn, a door of mystery which no key of earth can unlock. There is the hidden face of God, hidden from us, as it was from His own Son, when He cried in the lonely darkness of the cross, *Eloi, Eloi, lama sabachthani.* There are things that happen to us for which no explanation is vouchsafed, and for which none seems possible. In the journey of life we all find ourselves at some time or other confronted by the Sphinx of the desert, the inscrutable face with sightless eyes that stare right on, and the lips that utter nothing, and we hear the wind of the desert, and the prophets of the wind, who cry

> Hushed in the infinite dark at the end ye shall be
> Restless feverish souls that travail and yearn;
> Lo, we have lifted the Veil — there is nothing to see;
> Lo, we have looked on the Scroll — there was nothing
> to learn.

Elihu does not accept this despairing verdict, but he does argue that no perfect solution of the universe is possible, that mystery is necessary in the education of man, and that man was never meant to know, at least while upon the earth, the full explanation of God's ways, which are past finding out. And this leads him to a third thought which is implied rather than expressed, viz., the wisdom and joy of a complete surrender to God. "What is man that thou takest account of him," said the Hebrew Psalmist — for God does take account of man, and man is therefore safe with God. "I can look on terrible things with a steadier eye," says one of our modern prophets, "knowing as I do, that the world is not left to itself, but has a King who is its Redeemer." And to this truth Job himself assents when he says, "Though he slay me, yet will I trust in him"; he had then "reached his climax," he had found the quietness which God gives in the midst of trouble, and, while he dwelt in that refuge, no arrows of outrageous fortune had power to wound him. So then we see that the indisputable sovereignty of God is capable of being stated in a way very different from that of Omar, or Euripides, or Thomas Hardy. It makes not for despair, but for the peace that passeth all understanding. It lifts man out of the transient, and gives him safe anchorage in the eternal. It makes him say with one of the great and true poets of our time —

> It fortifies my soul to know
> That tho' I perish, Truth is so:
> That howso'er I stray or range,
> Whate'er I do, Thou dost not change,
> I steadier step when I recall,
> That, if I slip, Thou dost not fall.

In all lives there is the hidden thing which is signified in the darkened face of God, in all lives also there may be the divine quietness of faith; and it is on the truth of the Divine sovereignty that man bases all his faith, and enduring to the end is saved.

And now let us turn from the statement and discussion of these thoughts, which we all feel to be abstract and difficult, to the illustrations of them which we find in general human experience. The value of an abstract thought is its practical effect on human conduct. What effect on human conduct has this sublime thought of the sovereignty of God had: for of all philosophies as of all lives Christ's word holds true—"By their fruits ye shall know them."

Turn, for example, to the life of St. Paul. That life touched on agony of vicissitude which few lives have known, and a mere recital of its sorrows might appal the bravest. It knew hunger, thirst, and weariness, the alienation of friends, and the most murderous hatred of enemies; the loss of all things, and of the things that noble men value most, not goods and wealth, but honour, esteem, and respect: it knew physical suffering so intense that Paul spoke of himself as in deaths oft and dying daily: it knew a contempt from men so complete, that he says he had become as the offscouring of all things: it knew at last a violent death by martyrdom. The sufferings of Job, great as they were, are not comparable with the sufferings of Paul. And Paul knew also the withdrawn face of God, the denied prayer, the neglected appeal, the thorn in the flesh which caused him incurable and immitigable torture to his life's end. Yet you will find that the dominant note of Paul's life is triumph. He not merely does not complain of his sufferings, but he rejoices in them. His letters are not a tragic drama like the Book of Job: they are as the music of trumpets pealing round the dark dome of life, a sound of "harping symphonies and sevenfold hallelujahs!" And as you search his writings for the secret, you find it in the eighth chapter of his Epistle to the Romans—"Whom he did predestinate, them he also called: and whom he called, them he also justified: and whom he justified, them he also glorified. What shall we then say to these things? If God be for us, who can be against us?"

There you have the secret; the belief in the absolute sovereignty of God, the sense of the predetermined, and the consequent knowledge that nothing can happen to him for which God has not a reason, and a wise reason. He is God-inebriated, God-filled: lifted beyond the earth on wings of ecstasy: "sure of God as he is sure of life," and in a loftier language constantly repeats the saying of Elihu—"When God giveth quietness, who then can make trouble? if God be for us, who can be against us?"

A man may of course retort, and no doubt the question is already on our lips, but how can a man know that God is with him? The answer is that man may be with God, by a complete surrender to the will of God. "I hope God will be on our side," was a remark made to Abraham Lincoln, in the dark days when America was torn by fratricidal strife. "Sir," said Lincoln, "I have never yet asked myself whether God was on my side or not, but I tell you what, Sir, I am determined to be on God's side." And if any man asks me what is effectual calling, I say that you have the answer in that pregnant speech of Lincoln's. A man is on God's side who is on the side of truth, and righteousness, and virtue: for something in the bosom of the humblest man tells him that these things are dear to God. He is effectually called when he sets his soul on these things, and turns his face toward God's Zion. And those who are called, and obey the call, God shall justify: and those whom He justifies, He shall glorify. They who are upon God's side of truth, right, and virtue, alone have the right to say that God is for them. They alone grasp the secret of the Divine Sovereignty. And since all men can be upon God's side, if they will, all men may know the security and triumph of a peace which lifts them far above all the vicissitudes of earthly life, and teaches them to say out of the sacred silence of the sanctified and surrendered heart, "When God giveth quietness, who then shall make trouble?"

Turn again to history. It is not surprising that more and more the thoughts of cultured Englishmen are turned toward the great Puritan movement, for it gives us the key to all that is most vital and enduring in national character. But the more that movement is studied the clearer does it become that its political force was really incidental — its real force was religious. One need not recall the speeches of Cromwell, the despatches of Blake, the psalms sung upon the battlefield — these are things familiar to us: but they all illustrate one truth, the sense of the sovereignty of God which made the Puritan what he was. Those who see the Puritan only on the battlefield and in the council chamber see but one part of him: there is yet a nobler part portrayed in his religious experiences. It is no more than bare truth that Macaulay states of Puritanism when he says, "One overpowering sentiment had subjugated to itself pity and hatred, ambition and fear. Death had lost its terror and pleasure its charms. They had their smiles and their tears, their raptures and sorrows, but not for the things of this world. The intensity of their feelings on one subject made them tranquil on every other." On what subject we ask? On this tremendous subject of the sovereignty of God. If they cared little for kings, it was because they were devoted to the King of Kings and Lord of Lords: if they despised priests, it was because they knew themselves priests unto God by the mystery of a divine call, and a truer ordination. They also knew the mystery of the hidden face of God — and of that let the tears of Fleetwood, and the cries of Cromwell bear witness. They knew calamity: but they also knew how to triumph over it. John Milton knew the worst calamity that can happen to the man of letters — the total loss of sight; but he uttered no petulant complaint, and he might well have written the noble lines which a modern poet has put into his mouth; —

> I have naught to fear,
> This darkness is the shadow of Thy wing;
> Beneath it I am almost sacred: here
> Can come no evil thing.

And John Milton would have said, not by way of accusation, but in vindication of the ways of God with man, "Hath not the Potter power over the clay to do with it as He will?" The sense of the Divine sovereignty did not depress him: it inspired him. And it was the same with all the Puritans. The one subject on which their feelings were intense was the relation in which they stood to God: once sure of that, once convinced that God reigned and that they were called to be His children, His servants, and the sheep of His pasture — they were tranquil on every other subject, and could say, "When God giveth quietness, who then can make trouble?"

Or turn to modern biography, and recall the spiritual struggles of Carlyle, and the great emancipation which he won for himself, and for multitudes who through his words have been made wise unto salvation. He himself has told us how he won that emancipation; "God over all, God through all, and

God in us all" was the sum and substance of his Gospel. It is expressed again and again in all his works. When he rides by night past the old churchyard where the dead he loved were buried, an infinite peace comes upon him in the sense that God is over all. When the book on which he based all his hopes is burned, he speaks of the calamity as the chastisement of his invisible schoolmaster, and says, "What can I sorrowing do but obey — obey and think it the best!" When he writes his magnificent description of the night before the battle of Dunbar the same note makes itself heard —"The hoarse sea moans bodeful, swinging low and heavy against these whinstone bays: the sea and the tempest are abroad, and all else asleep but we — and there is One that rides upon the wings of the wind." The Divine Sovereignty once more: the steadfast sense that the world is rightly governed, that what we call histories and events is but God working — this was the strength of Carlyle's soul, it was upon this he based his life, and it is this conviction that has given him an influence on the best minds of the world, such as no other man since the days of the Hebrew prophets has wielded.

Or turn to modern imaginative literature. Much of it is mere coloured froth: some of it glitters with the iridescent hues of decay: but here and there a book emerges which is what a good book should be, "The precious life blood of a master spirit." Take up the *Window in Thrums*, for example, and turn to the pathetic sketch called *Dead this Twenty Years.* It is merely the account of a child who died by accident twenty years before, and the mother's thoughts about it all, and her grief. And this is what she says, "Thou God seest me," she exclaims. "Just when I came to 'Thou God seest me,' I let the book lie in my lap, for aince a body's sure o' that they're sure o' all: for I ken He was lookin' down when the cart gaed ower Joey, and He wanted to tak' my laddie to Himsel." And there is no other word said, or that can be said. To be sure that God reigns is to be sure of every thing, and when God giveth quietness, who then shall make trouble?

And so then we see that the one thought in which man can find comfort and repose in the day of sorrow, in the hour of unforeseen calamity, in the total wreck of human happiness, is this thought of the sovereignty of God. No doubt it is a thought that has been much misunderstood, abused, and misapplied: but the wisest and greatest of men have known how to use it and to stay their souls upon it. It is misunderstood when a man says of calamities which seem inexplicable, "They are good because they are the will of God." This is after all but another form of stoicism, and is not far removed from the sullen submission of the old pagan philosophers to a hierarchy of deities, whose government was caprice, whose will was tyranny, and whose ways were inscrutable. But it is rightly apprehended when a man says, "It is

God's will because it is good: because in some way unknown to me God seeks to discipline me, and because God is incapable of willing evil." When a man learns to say this he attains to the Divine quiet: peace descends upon him as a dew: alone, he is not alone; forsaken he is not forgotten; persecuted he is not destroyed, cast down he is not in despair; for over the sea of life by him uncharted, and along the ways of the sea to him unknown, there falls the voice of the Heavenly Steersman, who cries "*All's well.*" You and I have to face a life which is full of vicissitude. We know well enough that sorrows come upon us unexpectedly, and when we march most confidently to our Promised Land, we may find that our most tragic battle is yet to be fought. We cannot forget such things, and in our poor dumb, human way we often wonder how we shall meet such hours. Be sure of it mere human fortitude will not serve us then. Be sure of it stoicism will fail us, and no philosophic reconciliation to the inevitable will heal the wound that bleeds within. But one remedy for the troubled soul of man was never known to fail. Man can say, "God reigns — let God's will be done." He can realise that he is in the grasp of a mightier Power, who is not unloving, and that he is fulfilling a plan long predetermined. At every step of the way to his Calvary or his ascension, he may say as Jesus said, "The Son of man goeth, as it is written of him." Written where? In the inscrutable counsels of God to whom every life is known in its completeness before its first breath is drawn. You cannot read those counsels: "When God hideth His face, who then shall behold Him?" But you may know that He reigns, and reigns in wisdom, righteousness, and love, and then you will so far triumph as to say, "All is in God's hands, my trouble and my joy alike, and when He giveth quietness, who shall make trouble?"

And finally, the Book of Job declares the mystery of sorrow as solved in the mystery of Heaven. The Prologue gives us the key to the whole drama, when it shows Job's case as debated in heaven, and thoroughly understood there: the last act of the drama is the Divine intervention. A whirlwind once more blows, but not now to destroy, for God Himself rides upon its wings, and a Voice out of the whirlwind cries, "Whatsoever is under the whole heaven is mine." And again He cries, "Who is this that darkeneth counsel by words without knowledge?"

And at last Job replies, "I lay my hand upon my mouth. I have heard by the hearing of the ear: but now mine eye seeth thee." And behold the whirlwind passes and there is peace. Peace in the heavens that are as a sapphire for clearness, peace on the earth where the evening breeze begins to blow, and peace within the soul of Job. The dream of Heaven has come to him, with its promise of the very vision of God, its perfect knowledge, its solution of all earthly mystery; and because he is now sure of the Beneficent Sovereignty of God, he is able to believe that "there will come another era, when it shall be light, and man will awake from his lofty dreams to find his dream still there, and that nothing has gone save his sleep." O most dread and mighty Sovereign of the Earth and the Heavens, Thou who art the First and Last, the Beginning and the End, from whom nothing is hid, be it ours to serve Thee in humility, faithfulness, and truth, and so in the hour of trouble Thou shalt hide us in Thy pavilion, and when the dream of life is past, behold we shall awake in Thy image, and be satisfied.

FULFILMENT

IV

FULFILMENT

"That it might be fulfilled."—Matt. ii. 23.

THREE times in the course of eight verses do we come upon this phrase: it chimes upon the ear like the sound of a persistent bell. These eight verses narrate things which in themselves seem tragic and disastrous, and to which men would give the name of accident: but the Divine Word for them is *That it might be fulfilled.* They narrate the hurried and perilous flight into Egypt — the slaughter of the innocents, the return to Nazareth — each an incident wholly unforeseen, and surcharged with bitterness or sadness. Consider the pathetic picture of these anxious fugitives, with the Child of miracle upon their bosoms, driven out of Judæa by a great fear, flying for their lives upon an unknown path, until at last they see with tired eyes the Nile, the land of strange pyramids and vast temples, built ages before by the toiling slaves who were their ancestors; and does not that read like a tragic accident? Hear the voice of weeping and lamentation in Rama — must it not have seemed to many a mother who sat with a mangled babe upon her lap, that God was far away and forgetful of her sorrows? Consider the fugitives as they return, driven by the exigency of bread to dwell in a little town notorious for the godlessness and worthlessness of its inhabitants — and can Joseph and Mary discern, think you, any wise or beneficent end in such a fate? Yet each of these incidents was a link in a chain which bound eternity to time; it was a master-stroke of destiny; it was the result of predetermined and inevitable purpose; it all happened *That it might be fulfilled.* God was never nearer the world than in the hour when the cry of the bereaved mothers rose in Rama; never more surely at work in the shaping of human events than when these insignificant fugitives paused beside the Nile, or entered footsore and disheartened into Nazareth. Even the craft and wickedness of Herod yielded its quota to the establishment of prophecy, and without meaning or imagining it, Herod was obeying the prophets, and acting upon the compulsion of a Divine Providence. Is there, indeed, anything that happens in the world, any crime, or folly, or error of man's, that can be truly called accidental, an interruption or breaking away from the Divine order? Is not the very wickedness of man a contribution to the triumph of goodness, and like the wickedness of Herod, something that happens for the fulfilment of a larger scheme of goodness?

Now, here are three incidents in history: one, a

piece of painful human vicissitude — the second, a piece of horrible wickedness — the third, the sad irony of trouble which poverty is compelled to know, and each is set before us in no way accidental, but so far the reverse of accidental, that it is the unmistakable revelation of a Divine force working in the world. Perhaps the first thing we need to do is to understand our terms. Manifestly what is meant is not that Christ was carried into Egypt *because* Hosea predicted it; or that the children are slain *because* Jeremiah spoke of lamentation and great weeping in Rama: or that the infant grew up in Nazareth *because* the prophets spoke of a Divine Deliverer who should come out of Nazareth. To read the saying in this spirit would be to accuse Mary and Joseph of deliberate collusion, with an attempt to act a part, which is manifestly absurd; or which is little better, to suggest that things were bound to fall out as they did, simply because a Hebrew prophet had obscurely hinted at some such event. No: the truth lies in the reverse direction; the thing happened not because it was prophesied: but it was prophesied because it had to happen. For what is prophecy? It is two things, forth-telling and foretelling. The prophets were mainly forthtellers, and the great burden of their work was the exposition of great moral and spiritual truths. But ever and again, in some condition of spiritual ecstasy, they saw the clouds clear from the sky of the future, and caught momentary glimpses of the far-off dawn of a new time. They saw as men see in dreams, places, cities and countries, strangely vivid and real, and yet built of luminous mist and shadows only; they felt the incommunicable thrill of great events, linking themselves to such places, and heard the movements of the men and women who should inhabit them — and then they became foretellers. They had only a limited comprehension of their own words. They were unable to attach any quite definite meaning to them. They spoke as men speak in dreams, with vagueness and yet with a thrilling accent of truth. Those who heard them speak treasured their words, for they instinctively felt that there was a mystic meaning in them which some day would be made clear. Hosea had no actual vision of Christ in Egypt, Jeremiah no vivid and exact prevision of what it was that would make Rama a place of mourning; but each spoke in such a way, that when centuries afterwards certain things happened, men said, and said truly — "Behold the prophets said these things." Neither they, nor any since them, have understood what they really meant: but we know. To-day is this Scripture fulfilled; but it is fulfilled, not in arbitrary obedience to the word of a prophet, but the prophet spoke in obedience to a Divine instinct, he and we being both alike witnesses to the Divine order which rules the world. It is thus and thus alone that prophecy can become rational, intelligible, and a real communication of God made through the souls and minds of men.

But some one will very naturally say, "It is not so much with the nature of prophecy that we are concerned, as with the moral, personal, and theological questions involved in these statements. Take the personal question for example. Here is an obscure Jewish family driven into exile by the tyranny of Herod many centuries ago. Probably such a thing often happened in the days of Herod, who appears to have been one of the worst of rulers. But are we to believe that the actions of these men and women were of such consequence to the Supreme power, that it was well-known centuries before what they would do, and that what they did was done under the direct though unrecognised compulsion of the Almighty?" And to that question I reply, why not? Are *we* conscious of no compulsions of Providence? Are we not warned by our instincts in our dealings with one another, in our choice of the path we tread, in the sum of those small and large decisions which make up our destiny? Has no voice ever said to us, "this is the way — walk ye in it"; and has no voice told us that some other way our pride or ignorance would have chosen, was the way of peril or of death? And if we pass from the study of our own life to the lives of those who have bulked large before the world, who have done great things among their fellow men, and whose every stage of development and action is a matter of public scrutiny and general interest — is there any biography that does not teach the doctrine of divine compulsion as one of the best verified facts of life? Socrates may call it the voice of his dæmon, Knox may call it the voice of God, by Abraham Lincoln it is heard in dreams, by Luther in the whispers of the air; but is there any man who has ever attained to greatness as thinker or actor, who has not confessed that he has been the creature of mysterious compulsions, with a consciousness of moving in predetermined ways? And are not such confessions of a piece with the similar confessions of writers of the greatest genius, such as Milton and George Eliot, who have plainly stated that their very genius seemed not so much a thing of themselves, as the impartation to the mind of a message from the outside, by a species of Divine compulsion on the thought? *That it might be fulfilled* — the saying touches all lives. It is the confession alike of our glory and our impotence, and we have only to look within ourselves to find ample vindication of its truth.

But again it will be said, "That is not all; what about the moral question which is involved? One of the events in this chapter is a wanton and bloody massacre. It is, as you have said, a piece of horrible wickedness. It would no doubt be too absurd to suppose that it happened merely to give coherence and sense to a saying of Jeremiah; but is it possible to suppose that it happened at all by the permission of God? Does God recognise evil as a weapon for the carrying out of His designs, and can evil be recognised as a servant in the triumph of goodness?" And again I say, why not? For which is better, to think of evil as outside God's control or within it? Which is the more pious act of thought, to regard wickedness as something God cannot restrain, or as something perpetually defeated in its ultimate aims by the compulsion God puts upon it? And here again, does not the actual spectacle of life and history teach us something? This massacre in Rama was small and unnoticeable compared with the immolation of the Piedmontese, the slaughter of the Vaudois, and the barbarities of the Spaniards in the Netherlands, to say nothing of the martyrdoms of the early Christians. There have been times in human history, not so far away, when not a village or a district, but whole provinces and empires have wailed for their dead, and every house has been a house of mourning. There have been such wrongs wrought in outrage and spoliation that centuries have not been sufficient to wash out the stain of blood, or roll back the shadow that has fallen on a land. And in relation to such periods one of two statements is true: either God had abdicated the government of the world in these lurid reigns of blood, or God permitted them for a higher purpose; and the one statement ends in atheism as the other leads to faith and piety. But, as a matter of fact no competent historian has ever made the first statement. There can be no doubt that the surest possible weapon for the propagation of a religion is martyrdom. Such faith in Christ as Europe possesses to-day, such liberty of thought and reverence for truth, is the direct fruit of the days when the price of liberty was torture, and the crown of truth was death. For the final verdict on all such events — a verdict which cannot be delivered until ages have passed and historical perspectives have grown clear — is that in the long run truth only lives, and the wickedness of the wicked is compelled into the service of goodness and of truth. Herod does his work, but even he, in the very doing of his work, is fulfilling prophecy. The wailing in Rama is but the discordant tuning of the instruments in that divine orchestra which is presently to fill the world with an enduring music of love and hope. Wait till the discord dies away — then you will find its fulfilment in the larger music of eternity, which shall roll across the world, rousing it from its sleep, and creating a new soul under the very ribs of death.

But again it will be said —" What about the theological question? " In what does this differ from the doctrines of necessity and fatalism? Does it not lead directly to that saddest confession of the saddest poet of our time —

> If one is born a certain day on earth,
> All times and seasons tended to that birth,
> Not all the world could change or hinder it:
> I find no hint throughout the universe,
> Of good or ill, of blessing or of curse,
> I find alone necessity supreme.

In other and quite plain words, could Herod help what he did? And can the bad man who, by martyring the innocent, unconsciously but really works out the ultimate victory of the good — can he help playing the part he plays? Assuredly he can, for men are not mere puppets and blind mechanisms in the hand of God. A man who enters an express train is not responsible for its motion, but he is responsible for entering it. Once within it he must submit to its compulsion, and it is possible enough that it may carry him to some unintended bourne; but it was by his act, and his alone that he entered it. No: this is not fatalism, it is a very different thing; it is the statement of the real control of God over the world. Men act for one end, and God guides their action to quite another; men set their course, as the sailor does, and duly steer by it; but in every ocean there are tides and currents, winds and eddies that imperceptibly draw or drift the ship out of the exact course marked upon the map of man. We are undoubtedly free agents, and yet there is a law of gravitation which we obey every moment of our lives although we know nothing about it. And that then is the first and great point on which we fix our thoughts. It is not the veracity of the prophets that is being proved, it is the real sovereignty of God. It is not the correspondence between a saying of Jeremiah and the wickedness of Herod that is of interest, it is the fact of the real control of God over all human events. That which stands out large and luminous is the truth that compulsions of Providence touch every life; that we have relations to infinite forces of which we take small account; that our acts, which seem so intimately our own, are controlled and guided by a secret hand of which we are but dimly conscious; that God reigns over good and evil alike — unresting, unhasting, immutable — thwarted by no accident, deflected from His sovereign purposes by no revolt of man's — God reigns — and when the book of time is closed its final word will be — *That it might be fulfilled.*

But now, in the second place, let the mind dwell upon the word *fulfilled,* for in it is contained the mystery of hope of the Advent. What is fulfilment? The fruit is the fulfilment of the bloom, the meridian day is the fulfilment of the dawn. What we mean by the word as it is applied to Christ is, that there was something foreshadowed, and in Him that something was revealed; that on the lip of time there was a whisper and a suggestion, of which Christ was the uttered word; in the fulness of time "the Word became flesh and dwelt among us." How then, and in what way was Christ a fulfilment of foreshadowed things?

We find the answer in two directions: the first of which is that His person and His life fulfilled certain conditions long predicted. Let the minds of all who have the most casual knowledge of Scripture, range for a moment over the long series of predictions which by common consent have been applied to Jesus of Nazareth. They cover a vast period of time, and were uttered by a great variety of speakers. They are at once vague and definite. They become most precise in the mouth of Isaiah, who speaks of the lowly birth, the healing ministry, the sorrowful tragedy, the rejection, betrayal, and burial of One who is to bear the stripes wherewith we are healed, and to triumph by the force of virtue, meekness and love. Places and persons are named — "He is the Root of David," and His birthplace is Bethlehem. He is to prove something more than a local patriot: "He is the Desire of all Nations." His reign is to be widespread and everlasting: "He shall have the heathen for His heritage, and the uttermost parts of the earth for His possession." Through hundreds of years of Jewish history, this sublime figure was adumbrated to the Jewish mind. It is not pretended that either before or after Christ any other man fulfilled these conditions; and the proof of this statement is that the Jews still pray for the coming of

Him of whom Isaiah spoke. But in Jesus of Nazareth all these minute and manifold conditions were accurately fulfilled. Men did recognise in Him the long promised Messiah. He Himself, in the calm survey of His own career after His resurrection, asked whether the predicted Christ ought not to have suffered the things He suffered, and to have entered into His glory? I ask for nothing more than a rational and unbiassed consideration of these facts. Did these predictions mean anything or nothing? If they were true foreshadowings, who else is there who has in the least degree fulfilled these conditions? Where else in history is there any figure in whom all these predictions converge with such astonishing and perfect accuracy? I confess that for me there is nothing in human history so miraculous as this story, and the proof of its effect upon the human mind is that all the most cultured, enlightened, and civilized nations of the world have accepted Christianity and found in Jesus of Nazareth the long predicted and Divine Redeemer.

It was one of the beautiful and pathetic beliefs of the old Norsemen, quoted by Mr. Balfour in his *Foundation of Belief*, that when a man died his spirit survived him, and haunted as a ghost for a long time the scenes of his earthly life. "At first," says he, "vivid and almost lifelike, it slowly waned and faded, until at length it vanished, leaving behind it no trace or memory of its spectral presence among the throngs of living men." Let us reverse the legend, and then apply it to this subject. For long ages the faint adumbration of a divine deliverer haunted the minds of men. At first dim and spectral, the vision grew upon the minds of men, becoming with each age more definite and perfect. It fortified and invigorated the failing heart of the world with a new hope. Others besides Balaam learned to say, "I shall see Him but not now; I shall behold Him but not nigh. There shall come a Star out of Jacob, and a Sceptre shall rise out of Israel." Before the mind of a Plato as well as an Isaiah, this slowly growing vision passes, and each foresees the advent of some perfectly just One, by whom the world should be saved. Out of the films and spectral profundities of the future this face grew into clearness — this figure emerged into distinctness — until at last the spiritual and ghostly put on a human form, and God became flesh and dwelt among us. The dream was ended — the reality had come. Hope had fulfilled itself — faith was to begin. The vision was no more a vision; the palpable Redeemer spoke indeed "with man's voice by the marvellous sea," and stood before men with a human brow — and all this happened — *That it might be fulfilled.*

But the element of fulfilment is still more strikingly seen in the teaching of Christ. No one will venture to deny that long before the birth of Christ many pious and noble ideals of religion possessed the world, and not among the Jews alone. All that is meant by chastity, courage and fortitude, honour and duty and loyalty to truth, the subjugation of personal aims to public ideals, and a corresponding reverence for and service of the state, existed among the earlier Romans; and when we would learn and enforce these lessons to-day we can still find no nobler books than the literature with which Rome has furnished us. Nor can we forget that centuries before Christ a great religious revival had occurred in India, the main ethics of which were the mastery of the flesh, the complete sacrifice of the individual to the service of his fellows, and a noble passion to communicate the truths wherein spiritual freedom were found to all who would listen, irrespective of condition, state, or country. The very watchword of Rome was duty: the watchword of Buddha was still nobler — it was "delivered yourself, deliver others; and saved, make haste to save." It would be an ungrateful blasphemy against the Giver of all good and perfect gifts to deny or forget these things. But the more narrowly you examine the ancient religions of Rome and India, the more obvious is their lack of a true central element. They were not revelations of God: they could exist without God. With the Roman, morality was wholly divorced from piety — he went to the philosopher for his morals, and the priest for his religion. In Buddhism God did not appear; it was a religion of men toward men — the sublimest effort of pure altruism ever made by the unaided genius of man. But the greatest of all questions was overlooked — the problem of God received no solution. Was God magnanimous or merciful? Was it possible to love Him, or only to fear Him as an unexplained terror? That question was never answered perfectly till Christ came. But He answered it, and with His reply the world has been content. He fulfilled all of truth that was foreshadowed in the religions of Rome and India. He supplied the omitted, the neglected, element. He revealed the Father. At last the dumb lips of Time uttered more than a suggestive whisper — they spoke the living Word — and "we beheld His glory, the glory as of the only begotten of the Father, full of grace and truth." "I came," He said, "not to destroy but to fulfil" and with Him the gray dawn of truth passed into that perfect light which was the life of men — and all this happened that the sovereign will of God might be fulfilled.

And so then I come back to the great and vital truth of the real sovereignty of God over the world, with which we started.

Among many Oriental legends which gather round the temple of Solomon is one that has a touch of vivid significance — it is that Solomon died during the building of the Temple, but that his body remained leaning on a staff, and overlooking the workmen as though it were alive. Picture it, this gray and awful figure, forever rigid and immutable, there between the pinnacles of the Temple, with the first ray of morn, and there with the last star at night — spectral, terrible, lonely — toward which the trembling workmen turned fearful glances when the cloud lowered, or the light failed or the moon silvered all the earth with ghostly splendour! Picture the dead king, feared by the living workmen, who shrink from that dead eye which death himself cannot wholly close! It is a ghastly fancy, but not more ghastly than the thoughts men have had of God. For multitudes of men around us, God is but a dead Solomon: He has neither life, nor breath, nor motion. He is awful enough to impose some restraint upon the thought, but is as impotent as the dead King to impose restraint upon the conduct of men. He is but the dead figurehead of a forsaken universe. O my brethren, it is to deliver us from this most paralysing of all thoughts, that the incarnation took place. The birth of Christ is God's proof to us that He lives, that He rules, that He loves us. Until we believe with all our hearts in the real and vital sovereignty of God over this world of seeming turmoil and disorder, God is but a name to us, and religion but a habit of transmitted formalism. Look once more upon the whole scene — this fitting together of prediction and event — this overruling of evil for the work of infinite good, and learn that God reigns, and all these things happened that His will might be fulfilled.

And lastly, this truth of the real sovereignty of God I know not how to grasp, except as it is revealed to me in Jesus Christ. I can grasp the idea of a religion such as Rome knew; a certain Divinity in the State which demands my reverence, and constrains my duty. I can grasp the idea of a humanly altruistic religion such as Buddha taught, and the supreme need there is that I should love my fellow man better than myself if I am to justify my uses of existence. But I know not where to look for the revelation of a God to whom I can pray, whom I can adore and love, except in Jesus Christ. Some supreme Person in the universe I may suspect, but he may be dead as the dead king upon the roof of the unfinished temple for all I know. At the present hour perhaps this question of the real sovereignty of God may seem to have but a remote relation to your life. It may seem at best an abstruse and academic question. But the hour will surely come — in death if not earlier — when the supreme agony of your soul will sum itself up in the cry — does God live? Does God care anything for me? Am I anybody to God? God's reply to that deepest cry of humanity is Bethlehem. Immanuel — God with us — is the message of hope which the Church has gone on proclaiming for centuries — God with us in our pain, in our humiliations, in our lowest deeps of suffering, in our uttermost loneliness of death — God with us in our living and our dying — and we, by the grace of Christ's redemption with God for evermore, in the unknown felicity of eternal life. To know this is to know all that can be known of spiritual truth, to live by it is to realise all that can be realised of inward peace, for henceforth we can say, "God has been with us in the cradle and the grave — God has been for us in our extremity and distress — and if God be for us, who can be against us?"

TIMELESSNESS

V

TIMELESSNESS

"One day is with the Lord as a thousand years, and a thousand years as one day."—2 Peter iii. 8.

THIS passage affirms Timelessness as one of the attributes of God. The end and beginning are as one with Him. Space and period are non-existent. You can discover the beginning and the end of a line: but not of the circle; for the circle ends where it begins and begins where it ends. Perhaps this was the animating idea of Ezekiel in his strange imagery of the ever-revolving wheel full of eyes; he saw in the circle of the wheel the type of the unendingness of God.

Now to creatures finite and limited as we are, such thoughts and conceptions put an almost intolerable stress upon the mind. For, at first sight, it would appear, that Time is the ruling principle of the world. Seconds, minutes, days, months, years, centuries, epochs — it is by such measurements we take account of things. They are the milestones on the road of our existence. Our very life beats itself out by a pulse that registers its movements. The very sun moves in the harness of Time and obeys a punctual law. What then are we to make of that great opening clause of the prayer of Moses, the man of God, "Lord Thou hast been our dwelling place in all generations: from everlasting to everlasting, Thou art God?" Or, what of that strange paradox of the Psalmist —"In Thy book all my members were written, which in continuance were fashioned, when as yet there were none of them?"

Consider what these things imply; that we were nourished in the bosom of God's Everlasting before we knew the limits of Time; that in Him we were, when as yet we were not: that our substance existed in Him before it existed at all — as we understand existence. Well may we feel the stress put upon our thought as intolerable — but is not the one clear thing this, that for us also Time has no real existence, and a thousand years are as one day?

In such sayings human thought seems to overleap its own limits, and why? Let two facts, which are common to man, afford us the explanation. The first fact is, that to us the idea of anything without limit is terrible. It is this which lends an aspect of awfulness to the sea — it seems an unbounded immensity. We are easy in our minds when the shore is in sight, or not far away; but who has not been oppressed with a sense of something dreadful and lonely when he has sailed over its central depths, and reflected that those depths are from three to six miles, so that the highest mountain of the earth if dropped into the ocean would be utterly covered and forgotten as though it were a pebble thrown by the hand of a child upon the shore? The same thing affects us, but with increased intensity, when we gaze into a telescope, and see not only stars but tremendous chasms of space where no star shines, unlighted voids, the sites as it were of worlds either not yet created, or long since ruined and dispersed like such cities as Nineveh or Babylon. For the sky has its waste places, its infinitudes, and they are appalling. Looking into the depths of the heavens "there is a size," it has been said, "at which dignity begins: further on there is a size at which grandeur begins: further on there is a size at which awfulness begins: further on a size at which ghastliness begins." The imaginative powers confronted with such a spectacle simply bury themselves in the depths of a great horror. But whence this sense of horror? It is the horror of the illimitable. And it is even so we feel about God, when once we have grasped the idea of the illimitableness of God. From everlasting to everlasting Thou art God — it frightens us. With God a thousand years as one day — we shrink from the awfulness of the thought and say, How dreadful is this place! How natural is idolatry in the light of such a thought! How much easier to make an image of that which is unthinkable, and worship that — the plain, the tangible, the limited symbol of the illimitable. Was it not because idolatry is the natural act of man in the face of the illimitable that God put into the forefront of all His commandments to man this — Thou shalt not make a graven image nor bow down to it — I am that I am — and Me the eternal Present and Near, only shalt thou worship?

Again, when once we have put a limit to things our minds are at ease. It is something to know the boundaries, and depths of the ocean — at all events it is less terrible to us than to the Argonauts, and the early voyagers and discoverers, who were the first to break into the silent sea. The horror is gone when we know the limit. It is the same with astronomy. We may take its enormous figures — and tell ourselves that the light moves at the rate of twelve million miles a minute: that the sun and all the solar system is rushing onward to a certain point in the constellation of Hercules at the rate of thirty-three million miles a year; and that it will reach that fixed terminus in a little less than two million years. Such figures are almost unthinkable — nevertheless they do not alarm us. And why? Because they *are* figures — because they put a limit on things. After a while it becomes as easy to say thirty-three millions, as one, two, three. The rest is merely a matter of multiplication, and we find peace of mind in our arithmetic. But from everlasting to everlasting — the timeless, the boundless, the illimitable — it is that which appals and frightens us. One day as a thousand years

— it seems as if the centre of gravity in all our thought were lost — and we are dumb not only with perplexity, but with a nameless awe.

Here then is the first practical truth on which we may lean. You ask of God a task nearly unthinkable — that He shall number the hairs on the head of every human creature, and that no multitudinous sparrow shall fall to the ground without His knowledge. You ask really far more than that even; that not the least creature in all His worlds shall be beyond His cognisance and care. For who can doubt that the innumerous stars we see above us are inhabited? It would be a strange thing indeed if among all these rushing worlds only one, and that the least, had inhabitants. And it would be still more inconceivable that if they are inhabited, God cares only for the people of the earth, and neither knows nor cares for anything beyond this one troubled star. In other words, if the very hairs on the heads of men are numbered, it is a necessity of thought that no less can be said or imagined of the peoples of a million stars, the distant light alone of which is known to us. How can such a task be accomplished? Only by One who is timeless, boundless, illimitable. *He* might do it — no other. For if there be a limit anywhere with God the whole thought breaks down — I may be outside that limit as truly as the humblest creature of the furthest star, and for all I know I am without it. If God can overlook a world how much easier to overlook me! So then, the one foothold and certainty of faith is in this illimitability of God, and we express not only our own faith, but the faith of all the worlds, when we say, "From everlasting to everlasting — Thou art God!" This is indeed the creed of the universe, rehearsing which the sons of God shout for joy, and the morning stars sing together.

But let us turn to another phase of the thought. We have admitted that all our thoughts and conceptions are governed by the sense of Time: yet do we not find that Timelessness also enters into our own life? There are occasions in all human life, when that strong apocalyptic angel who stands upon the sea and upon the earth — upon the intangible and the tangible, the fluid and the fixed — lifts his hand to heaven, and swears by Him that liveth for ever and ever, that Time shall be no more. What occasions are these? Have we ever known them? Let us name and examine two only.

First, imagination is Timeless. In the flash of an instant, and the least conceivable fraction of an instant, I am with Adam in Eden, I see the waters of the flood, I experience all of the thrill and passion of

> Old, unhappy, far-off things,
> And battles long ago.

Light may travel swiftly; but I can outspeed the light. I may talk of centuries — but they are mere forms and conveniences of speech — they mean nothing. The scholar lives not in the university of Oxford — he lives with Homer in old Greece: the historian of the Roman Empire lives not at Lausanne but under the shadow of the Coliseum. Men saw Gibbon writing in that old garden at Lausanne but it was only his corporeal frame they saw — his mind was far away. For the historian, life has no tenses — the imagination has destroyed them. Here, at least, it becomes literally true for all of us that a thousand years are as one day — and that while Time may regulate our clocks, it cannot put the least hindrance on our spirits, or on the life of our minds.

In the same way it is true that emotion is Timeless. "It seems but yesterday," says the old man as he talks of his early life: and it is but yesterday, for Time is to him in such a solemn moment of reminiscence, as though it were not. "The pain is as keen to-day as it ever was," says the mourner: undoubtedly, for Time has no jurisdiction over sorrow. It is many years since the mother or the child died: but have years done anything to make the loss less real? Do we not still wake in the night and see it all, feel it all again: the pang of heart with which we read the tragic telegram, the hasty journey, the agony of impatience, the trembling hand upon the door, the whispered word, the pale face upon the pillow, the dim light, the eyes that met ours in an ineffable yearning — the very smell of sickness, and the merest trifles of the room, such as the watch ticking beside the bed, and the text of Scripture on the wall? What has Time to do with such poignant experiences as these? Absolutely nothing. We have passed into the limitless. If we live beyond the earth, we think these things will still live in us. And of this we are sure, that for those who have passed beyond the earth love still lives, and Time and Space are powerless to destroy it. Does not every true lover, for whom love is of the soul, feel and acquiesce in the solemn pathos and faith of the dying Pompilia's speech in Browning's, "*Ring and the Book* ":

> In heaven we have the real and true, and sure,
> 'Tis there they neither marry nor are given
> In marriage but are as the angels: right,
> O how right that is, how like Jesus Christ
> To say that! . . .
> Be as the angels rather, who, apart,
> Know themselves into one, are found at length
> Married, but marry never, no, nor give
> In marriage.
> So, let him wait, God's instant men call years.

"God's instant men call years "— that which was, and is and will be — and is not that also saying that with God a thousand years are as one day; and with us too, when we feel ourselves to be not perishable bodies, but imperishable and immortal spirits? Time does not breathe indeed on the fadeless bloom of this world of the emotions — and it is the angel of love, of deathless tenderness and passion who swears by Him who liveth for ever, that Time shall be no more.

What is it then that we ascertain by the contemplation of such a fact as this? It is that Time regulates our outer life but it has no power over our mind. It is that whether we recognise it or not there is an immortal part in us, even as the wise writer of Ecclesiastes said, "also God hath set eternity in the heart of man." It is that beyond all other things we see that love knows nothing of Time — for the love we had for the dead mother or the child we still have — not a pang is lost, not a kiss forgotten: years have altered nothing, for "love is not love that alteration knows." Now see then how things fit in with this truth. What is God? God is love, is the sublime reply. What is love? Love is an emotion without limit; it knows neither past nor future; it is an eternal Now.

Do we complain of our insignificance, our distance from God, and the impossibility of God knowing anything of us? Time, distance, space, nearness, farness, have no existence with God. They have no existence with love. The whole breadth of the world may yawn between us and the one human creature we love best: but it has no effect on our love. Infinite vastness may intrude itself between us and God: it has no effect upon His love. In that eternal Now of the divine love all men are included: nay all creatures are included too: for the saying of Christ is not only that the very hairs of our head are all numbered, but that not a sparrow falls to the ground — its tiny song stilled, its infinitesimal spark of life extinguished — without the Father.

There are many expressions in the Bible which seem to us entirely inscrutable. Thus, when Jesus pronounces the blessing of the faithful servants, He says, "Inherit the Kingdom prepared for you *from the foundation of the world.*" In His great sacramental prayer our Lord prays that His disciples may know the love wherewith God loved Him *before the foundation of the world.* St. Paul speaks of those who were chosen in God *before the foundation of the world;* and St. John speaks of the Lamb who was slain *from the foundation of the world.* What can these words mean? Is not this an even more perplexing paradox than the Psalmist's when he speaks of his members being fashioned when as yet there were none of them? How can men be loved before they exist, and Christ be slain before He is born? The answer once more is that God is the I Am — the eternal present tense — the Alpha and Omega, the beginning and the end. There is no *to be* with God — all *is.* Past and present run together, and are annihilated in Him. The Cross was from eternity, the love from eternity, and the Lamb is not slain at some period of Time that we can name, but from the foundation of the world. In the eternal day of the Most High there is neither dawn nor night — it is one sacred high eternal noon, and a thousand years are but as one day.

But this is not all. Think yet again: do we not discover in such expressions the hint of some real correspondence of nature between man and God? To be known, chosen, and loved before the foundation of the world must mean, if it mean anything, that there is something in us that existed before the foundation of the world, and will out-last it. For the Psalmist speaks only of his physical frame, his members as written in the book of God before they were fashioned: what was it God loved in him then in the day when he was not so far as his earthly part was concerned? Manifestly the soul. And there at last we reach the clue which threads the mystery: we were all souls before we were bodies, and we shall still be souls, when our bodies have returned to dust. And for the soul Time does not exist, nor space, nor nearness, nor farness: and the love of God to man is the immortal embracing the immortal, that which always was, communing with that which always was and is: the Timeless locked in eternal fellowship with the Timeless. "Thou art from everlasting to everlasting — we shall not die"— cried the Hebrew prophet: no, because we also live and move in the everlasting Now of the Highest. O, man, living for nothing beyond the day, seeing all things as bounded by the mean horizon of Time, hear this: thou wert before the foundation of the world, and thou wilt be when the world has passed away! There is no such thing as the horizon — we know well enough that it is a mere optical delusion. That blue rim and edge of the world you think you see is no rim — it is the abyss. Travel toward it — you cannot reach it; try to touch it — it is not. A mirage, an hallucination only — that is all it is: and Time itself is even such an hallucination. Our life knows abysses but no horizons: our troubled years are but a moment in the everlasting Being: and for us also a thousand years are as one day.

I admit that language toils in vain to express these things: that they are philosophical truths which almost exceed comprehension: and if they were only philosophical truths I would not occupy my time or yours in the effort to expound them. Even now some of you may be saying, Why not preach something quite plain and practical, which has a clear and cogent bearing on the daily life of a tired business man? But these are not merely philosophical truths — pray can you tell me of any truth that has so searching, cogent, and practical a bearing on the daily life of the tired man of business as this truth which assures him that he has a soul? For that is just what such a man is most apt to forget. Time governs all his thoughts — Time is money — Time seems a very real horizon imprisoning his energies, and he is apt to become the merest slave and drudge of Time. Who then needs so much to be told that the horizon is not real, that for the soul there is no such thing as Time, and that he has a soul fashioned after the image of God, and loved by God before the foundation of the world? Does it not alter all things to believe that? Can a man who believes it drudge his life out to make money, without a single higher purpose: can he be prayerless, undevout, unthinking, grudging to God one poor hour of worship in a week and attending public worship more from habit than from instinct? And besides, have we not already seen that this tremendous thought of man's personal relation to God is the most powerful of all thoughts in shaping character: that it has convulsed and regenerated nations: that it has imposed on man a sense of responsibility which has had more to do with the shaping of civilisation than anything else: that it has produced literatures, launched armies, given stability to human government, and again and again, bred the hero of liberty and martyr of truth? We cannot ignore such facts. Tell a man Time is all he has, and dust all he is: and he will behave as the beasts that perish, and even worse than they. Tell him that he is the true child of the Eternal, and all life is altered to him. The horizon of Time has vanished, the heaven is opened to him, and all his life will be lived as in the sight of Him, whose he is, and whom he serves.

"And, Lo, I am with you always even to the end of the world," says Christ in His sublime farewell to His disciples. Once more see how all things fit in with these truths. For Christ thus proclaims *Himself* from everlasting to everlasting. In this world to which He came for a season, He also moved within the horizon of Time — and He spake of His hour — "My hour is not yet come": once beyond it He had reached the realm of the Timeless — no hours — no periods — it is *I Am* — and it is *always*. I have already said that there are states of feeling which we all know, and which are outside the jurisdiction of Time. Jesus Himself has provided us with one sacred form of service, the very essence and meaning of which is that it takes us quite outside the limits of Time. At the table of the Lord we pass into Timelessness by the force of faith and love. Our emotion annihilates the years and centuries, and we go back in the flash of an instant to that guest-chamber where the Redeemer sits, and says: "Do this in remembrance of Me." Our faith does more: we feel the living embrace, we hear the living voice of Him who is alive for evermore, and we know Him with us in the breaking of bread. He who was slain before the foundation of the world loves us who existed, in the purpose of God, before the foundation of the world. Not only the horizon of Time, but the horizon of sense also has melted away — and there is a Real Presence indeed, and "Spirit with spirit can meet, Closer is He than breathing, and nearer than hands and feet." Child of Time and earth, draw near, and know thyself for what thou art — the child of God, loved from the foundation of the world with an everlasting love. Know thy Saviour for what He is — slain for thee, and with thee in the undying life of the Spirit, always, to the end of the world. Know the Spirit of God the Comforter as thine: the breath of the Eternal perpetually breathed into thy spirit, and renewing it. And, knowing all this, join in the great Antiphon of faith and praise — love and adoration:

Glory be to the Father, and to the Son, and to the Holy Ghost. As it was in the beginning, is now and ever shall be, world without end. Amen.

GOD'S POEMS

VI

GOD'S POEMS

"For we are his workmanship, created in Christ Jesus unto good works, which God hath before ordained that we should walk in them."—Eph. ii. 10.

THE contention of Paul in this passage is that men and women are not the sole architects of their own characters—the Supreme Architect who works upon them is God. We are saved by grace—by a long series of Divine interpositions, by Heavenly compulsions and impulsions, by the energies of a ceaseless Hand that works upon us and brings out the Heavenly design, and completes the Divine symmetry. Is there any one of us who has not made that discovery? Are there not moments when the most self-reliant of us is made to feel that he is in the hand of God, that all our purposes in life and really noble efforts after completeness of character are touched with a humbling inefficiency—that, in fact, anything of goodness in us is not a rare plant that we have brought to birth, but the flower of a rare seed that an unseen hand has sown in us, and nurtured? It is easy, of course, to turn such a thought into folly. Human nature is, unfortunately, so constituted that very few minds are capable of seeing both sides of a truth. Thus it happens that those who cling most to the consoling thought of a gospel of pure grace often neglect the equally binding gospel of a ceaseless struggle after goodness. And again, the good people who build up a life of flawless honour, integrity, and virtue, often find, because they have not learned to need it, a gospel of grace incomprehensible. Yet both are true, just as it is true that a ship depends for its movement equally on the men who work the pulleys and the wind that fills the sails. So we work out our own salvation; but we wait the Divine wind, that blows as it listeth, and we move to no heavenly shores till the wind comes out of the waste heaven, and God touches us. For it is by grace, by a Divine interference, that we are saved; nor is there salvation possible without it.

I do not often dwell upon this mystic side of religion, because, as I conceive the spirit of modern life, few of us are able to bear it. We are tempted by so many tendencies of modern life to indifference in religion that our natural spiritual indolence would only be increased tenfold by the doctrine that salvation is all achieved for us. In the age of monasticism, when men and women were seeking to work out their salvation by endless acts of penance, charity, self-renunciation, and ritual obedience, it was a great spiritual discovery to tell men they were saved not of themselves, but by the overwhelming interposition of God. Such a truth, as it was uttered by Luther, marked the hour of daybreak in Europe; as it was uttered later on by Wesley, resulted in the resurgence of all the deep springs of spiritual life which had been sealed for many generations in England. It was this supreme truth that converted both Luther and Wesley, and the one rose from Pilate's staircase in Rome with the dawn upon his brow, as a man enfranchised of a new world: the other in Aldersgate Street in half-an-hour cast the husk of twenty years of ritualism, and emerged into unbounded spiritual liberty. For us also to grasp this truth is life. Yet so ill-balanced and frail of judgment are we that there is only too much peril of wresting such a truth to our destruction. Rather for us the most necessary truth to-day is that goodness can only be found by effort, that the Kingdom of Heaven suffereth violence, that God will not save us by any spiritual necromancy, that if we are not prepared to be as earnest over religion as we are over our worldly affairs, there is no religion and no salvation for us. When men are seeking to be saved by a wrong method, yet are in deadly and consuming earnest over it, as men were when they left all to go on painful pilgrimages to the shrines of saints, it is time to say, "Poor soul, look up. You will never save yourself; but Christ saves you, and all out of free grace." But when men take no count of religion, beyond giving it two or three indolent hours on the Sunday: when they care far more for a rise in stocks or a turn in the market than for Heaven or Hell, it would be folly to foster their indifference by saying, "You need do nothing to be saved; you are saved by grace." And it would be untrue to say it. There is much that we must do before we can hear the voice which assures us that there is a gospel of grace that makes good our deficiencies and does for us what we could not do for ourselves. It is only when we have fulfilled the gospel of works that we have any right to comfort ourselves with the gospel of grace, for it is only then that we can receive it without injury, and rest in God for final salvation because we are co-workers with God in achieving our redemption.

But the beauty and suggestiveness of this passage lies in the use of a single word which is altogether inadequately rendered in our version. Translators and scholars are seldom men of imagination, and when a fine word is given them, as is the case here, they usually fail to use it — fail for lack of imagination. We are His workmanship, His handicraft: it is a good enough word, but is not Paul's word. Paul's word is we are *His Poems.* Now what is a poem? It is the finest flower of the finest mind. It is only once or twice in a century that Nature is able to produce the mind which has such a happy equipoise of faculty that its expression is poetry. It is only now and again that even a great poet produces a true poem, which enters into the mind and memory of the world. Biographers of Wordsworth have marked the exact period when his genius reached its height, and after that the glory came only at intervals, and the real poems were rare. And because a true poem is so rare a thing, it has always been appraised as the highest form of literature. Many great books come — and go, but a true poem is as fresh after long centuries as when it was first written. "Poesy never waxeth old," and knows no decay. It knows no decay because it is permeated with the spirit of beauty: because it is the enduring monument of a combination of fine gifts, whose final result is a thing of beauty and a joy for ever. That is what a poem is, and St. Paul says that we are the expression of the mind of God, as the *In Memoriam* is the expression of the full mind and heart of Tennyson: We are *God's Poems.*

But this very comparison opens another depth of thought. Suppose Paul had said — We are God's histories. That would have been equally true, for God has written Himself upon the tablets of empire and the fields of battle where human history is made. But there is this difference between a poem and a history: the one is the personal expression of a man's soul; the other is simply the work of a man's mind. The historian is not required to express himself; on the contrary, he is required to leave himself out of the question, that he may write his history with an unbiassed vision. But the poem depends entirely upon the poet for its creation. It is the unveiling of the deepest and most intimate secrecies of his heart. His own image is projected over every page, and it is the poignant personal element in poetry that makes it so beautiful, and gives it its enduring charm. Men, then, are God's Poems. The intimacies of God's heart are expressed in man: God's highest thoughts, God's deepest emotions. The prayer of Moses was that the beauty of God might rest upon him; when a man is finished at last in the likeness of Christ, God's sense of beauty is satisfied in him, God's art has found its finest expression and the beauty of God does rest upon him. The true Christian is God's Poem in a world of prose; God's beauty in a world of gloom: God's fine and finished art, in a world where men forget beauty, and are careless of moral symmetry and spiritual grace.

There are two directions in which we catch some glimpse of these truths: we can readily believe that little children are God's Poems, and that in the life which completes itself in moral unity, there is a touch of Divine poetry. Childhood is itself the poetry of life, and many a man whose soul has been thrilled with the charm of little children, has said with Longfellow: —

> You are better than all the ballads
> That ever were sung or said,

For you are the living poems
And all the rest are dead.

If God indeed looks down on earth and smiles, children are His smiles; if He indeed is a Poet, these are His Poems. And so, also, when we see the rare spectacle of a life that from first to last is governed by high thoughts, moves on a high level, is held together by a noble unity of design and effort, we can see that this life is like a gleam of noble poetry on the dull page of life. Look then at these things, and you will understand Paul's words — We are God's Poems. Christianity gives back to life its first fresh childlikeness, and says we must be as little children; it gives the fine unity of the noblest aim to the life that obeys its mandate. Christ works out by His indwelling the image of true beauty in us, so that, at the last, we move through the throngs of men with a light that never was on sea or land upon us, a charm akin to the exquisite and indefinable charm of poetry, for in truth we have become God's Poems, and are the thought of God interpreted in human forms.

But not only in the child, and in the life that manifests a real and noble unity, do we gather the suggestion of this passage; have we not also seen the concrete examples of what is meant in men and women we have known? When Carlyle describes Elizabeth Fry standing fair as a lily, in pure womanliness, amid the abominable sights of old Newgate;

or Longfellow describes Florence Nightingale moving with her lamp among the wounded at Scutari —

> And slow, as in a dream of bliss
> The speechless sufferer turns to kiss
> Her shadow, as it falls
> Along the darkening walls —

what is the effect on the mind? It is the effect of poetry. We feel touched, purged, exalted: we know that these women were in truth God's Poems. And there are men and women in the world still who touch the soul by the same Divine magic. We feel better for having seen them; the air is sweetened when they come; the mind finds joy in them, and the heart is rested. When a man like this enters the home of sorrow, the sunshine comes in with him; when such a woman enters a room full of vain, worldly, and frivolous people, the range of thought is instantly raised, and the whole atmosphere of the room is purged and freshened. God's poetry has interrupted for a time the prose of life. We have felt as though a shining presence had been with us, and our poor sordid pleasure-seeking life has felt strangely mean to us. That is precisely the effect of poetry, it lifts us into a higher world; that also is the effect of the man or woman in whom Christ dwells — they make the poetry of life and move through the world to the sound of far-off music, that floats in wind-borne harmonies into the hearts of the least sensitive.

There is no more difficulty in recognising these living poems than there is in feeling the difference between poetry and prose. Jesus Christ was God's great and perfect Poem, and He sets the standard of perfection; and as we are like Him, so do we reach a higher image and become the Poems of God.

And so we touch a yet deeper truth — the God who wrought the perfect Poem of Jesus Christ is still creating and finishing His Poems — not copies, mark you; not mere echoes, but new Poems — complete and individual, though all conforming to the type of beauty Christ has given us. The usual, because the easiest, way of preaching Christ is to preach Him as an example, and to tell men to copy Him. It is right as far as it goes, but it does not go far enough. We need to copy Christ, to compare our conduct with His, to measure our motive by His ideal; and even John Stuart Mill said there was no finer law of conduct than to ask how Christ would have acted and spoken in any difficult set of circumstances which we may encounter. But does the man who copies Raphael become a Raphael? Does the man who moulds his music on the Tennysonian melody become a Tennyson? Where in art or letters do we find the copyist ever treated with respect? By what is art or poetry richer for the laborious copies of Raphael or Rubens, or the slavish echoes of Elizabethan or Tennysonian poetry, which have filled the reams of unsold books, or acres of unmarketable canvas? And neither is it the end of Christianity to fill the world with weak copies of Christ. The phonograph can retain the inflections of the human voice, and reproduce them, but after all it is not the human voice. To hear Bryan speak or Nordica sing is a very different thing from hearing the thin reduplication and echo of their voices through the phonograph. It may be claimed that the echo is exact; that inflection by inflection, it utters the very words that eloquent or lyric lips have uttered; but one word from the living lip is worth all that the phonograph can ever give us. No; Christianity aims at nothing less than to make us new and living Christs in this world of the twentieth century, spreading the same influence, living in the same temper, ready to suffer and die in the same spirit as Jesus did centuries ago in Palestine. It claims not to make copies but creations. It claims not to stamp new patterns on old cloth, but to make all things new. It does not merely change a man, it transforms him into a new image. It produces not slavish echoes of the great poetry of Christ, but Poems — men and women in whom again God utters Himself, and expresses His infinite Art.

Let us then gather up the practical lessons of the thought.

And the first is that such a magnificent conception of what a man may be should be at once a restraint and impulse to us. Who can think meanly of life or of himself with such a phrase ringing in his mind? And the commonest temptation of life, especially in great cities, is not to think too highly of ourselves but too meanly. We are likelier to perish by despondence than by pride, by self-contempt than vanity. We are daily tempted by the very multitudinousness of life to think poorly of our own opportunities, to tell ourselves that great ideals are not possible for such as we are, that the heights are out of reach, that for us the poetry of life is a closed book, a denied and forfeited delight. And when men think thus, what wonder is it that they act poorly? What marvel that they permit the growth of narrowness and poor-spiritedness in themselves, that they learn to do mean things and tread in sordid ways, that they cease to care anything for the dignity of life, and in mind and morals become slovenly and careless, till last of all they fall out of the range of the wisest and best voices, and hear them no more, nor regret their loss? It is in such hours we need to remind ourselves of the dignity of life, and that man was at first, and still may be, God's Poem. We all know how Carlyle vituperated at what he called Darwin's "gorilla damnifications of humanity," and ethically he was right. Man does not need to be told of the depth from which he has sprung, but of the height to which he may reach. He needs to hear less of the descent of man and more of the ascent of man through Jesus Christ. When you are tempted to let your ideals of youth slip out of sight, to give up the pursuit of excellence and turn from the difficult path that leads to life, to take a poor mean-spirited view of life and live in accordance with it, here then is your sovereign remedy; look to Christ and see what He was, how He lived, what He is to the world to-day, and remember that you, too, may be a Poem of God, created in Christ Jesus unto good works.

To do this will also help you to think well of all men. There are many men in the world who are illegible poems — illegible to us who can see no element of God's poetry in them, yet not one of them is utterly without the faint outlines of God's intention visible in him. To us the early Saxon poetry is practically unintelligible; but when a scholar takes it up, and fits piece to piece, and finds the sequence of thought and rhythm, it becomes at once noble poetry, the force and fulness of which all can feel. Let us think of our brother man in the same spirit. Nay, more, let us think of the world itself as a Poem that is still being written, and which will at the last be worthy of the art of God. Hope for ourselves; Hope for our brother man; Hope for the world; that is the true Christian spirit. Believe that God's will is being done; that He is still working in the world; that He must conquer; that every day is really bringing us nearer to the new earth wherein dwelleth righteousness.

More than once in those long nights I spent on the Atlantic, I went on deck when all was still, and felt how insignificant a thing was man, in all that lonely immensity of sea and sky. There was no sound save the cry of the wind among the spars, the throb of the great engines, the sound of the many waters rushing round the vessel's keel. I felt the mystery of life; I was conscious of "the whisper and moan and wonder and diapason of the sea." And then out of the stillness there came a voice, clear and ringing — the voice of the man on the look-out crying to the night, "All's well, and the lights burn bright! All's well, and the lights burn bright!" How did I know all was well? What knew I of the forces that were bridled in the mysterious throbbing heart of those unceasing engines, of the peril that glared on me in the breaking wave, or lay hidden in the dark cloud that lay along the horizon? I knew nothing; but the voice went sounding on over the sea: "All's well, and the lights burn bright!" And the wind carried it away across the waters, and it palpitated round the world, and it went up soaring and trembling, in ever fainter reverberations, among the stars. So I stand for a little while amid great forces of which I know little; but I am not alone in the empty night. The world moves on to some appointed goal, though by what paths I know not;

it has its Steersman, and it will arrive. And, amid the loneliness and mystery, the peril and uncertainty, I have learned to hear a Voice that cries, "All's well!" and tells me why all is well; it is the Voice of Christ saying, "Lo, I am with you always, even to the end of the world." God has not left His world. He is working out His supreme Art in it every day, and if we be true Christians we are God's Poems wrought in Christ Jesus unto good works.

ELIJAH'S LONELINESS

VII

ELIJAH'S LONELINESS

"And he said, I have been very jealous for the Lord God of hosts: for the children of Israel have forsaken thy covenant, thrown down thine altars, and slain thy prophets with the sword; and I, even I only, am left; and they seek my life to take it away."— I Kings xix. 10.

IN the lives of all great men there come hours of spiritual crisis, which are often inexplicable in their origin and tragic in their results. Brave men are swept away by sudden tides of cowardice, heroic men know the ignominy of fear and the agony of despondence. No character is built upon quite simple lines: often it is the coherence of antagonistic tendencies — as we see in John, who was the apostle of love and yet is the very type of intolerance; of Peter, who is the bravest of the brave, and yet was thrice a coward and a liar. We are all conscious, if we take any care to observe ourselves, of sudden lowerings of spiritual temperature, of nameless movements in our own hearts, out of which, as out of the stirring of a wind, comes a gray cloud that spreads itself over the firmament of life. It is such an hour in the life of Elijah. The passion and excitement of the great scene on Carmel have passed away. The re-action is upon him. He is fugitive and foodless, and the faintness of despair spreads itself through his heart. He magnifies his own sensations till every detail stands out in gigantic emphasis: he is alone on the side of right, and the whole world is leagued against him. Do not we in the same manner, in our hours of despondence, set out all our feelings, our failures, our broken ambitions in the same gigantic array, till we persuade ourselves that none have drunk as bitter cups as we, none have been so hardly used, so little valued, so unjustly scorned! We even persuade ourselves that death is sweet, and with a bitter daring we call on the last hour to come and put an end to us. The keynote of such a condition is an exaggerated egoism: it is only in such hours of hurt vanity, and wounded pride, that we cry —"O Lord, take away my life, for I am not better than my fathers."

But if we look a little closer we shall see that there is something more than hurt egoism here, and something deeper. What is this sorrow that weighs so heavily on so great a heart as Elijah's, that he calls for the angel of the last hour to give him ease? It is the sorrow of an overwhelming loneliness, it is such a loneliness as Shelley has pictured in immortal verse:

> Alas, I have nor hope, nor health,
> Nor peace within, nor calm around,
> Nor that content surpassing wealth,

The sage in meditation found,
And walked with inward glory crowned.
Nor fame, nor power, nor love, nor leisure,
Others I see whom these surround,
Smiling they live, and call life pleasure,
To me that cup has been dealt in another measure;
I could lie down like a tired child,
And weep away the life of care,
Which I have borne, and yet must bear.

It is the sense that no one sympathises with our deepest thoughts, that our ideals are not the ideals of the world, that our best actions are misconstrued, our best gifts fail equally of recognition and reward. Life is not dealt in this measure to others — this is the bitterness of it. Ahab and Jezebel and the careless and sensual crowd who gather in the flower-decked temples of Baal find a joy in life which is denied to you. Thousands of people pass you in the street who find restfulness even in the dulness of their lives, because they have no aims beyond the satisfaction of the meanest desires. You would fain do great things for the world, and you can do nothing. You follow the gleam of a vision others do not see; or hear of, only to deride. You do not even gain the vision yourself — it is but a troublous glimpse, as of a star swimming for an instant into a little lake of blue between heavy clouds. What is the use of trying? O Lord, take away my life, for I am not better than my fathers! Every man who aspires after high things feels thus: if we have not felt it, it is because we have never known such aspiration.

Loneliness is the commonest of all human miseries, and if we are to understand this phase of Elijah's life, and the cure of it, let us begin by admitting this fact. In the plainest sense of the word we are lonely, and cannot be otherwise. Those who know and love us best know not half the reasons why we sigh or smile. Men and women may live together in what seems the closest intimacy for years, and yet keep within their hearts reserved and barriered chambers to which neither has the key. Children may grow up in a home, and yet be utterly alien in the deeper things of the spirit. Our life may be spent among crowds, and yet the vast silence which encloses the heart may never once be broken. For many of us the effort to explain ourselves is impossible; when we would fain speak a fatal reticence seals our lips, and the golden hour passes and never comes again. For others among us the golden hour never strikes. As life passes out of that season when confidences are most easily exchanged, we are more and more driven back upon ourselves. It pains us to see the ease with which others seem to find an apparent unity of life, because for us it seems always out of reach. Have we not all felt how true this is? Do I, who am your friend and minister, know your lives — your real inward lives — in any but the most superficial way? Do you know mine? Is not every word of comfort or counsel uttered from the pulpit a bow drawn at a venture, for who can tell where is the heart to whom it appeals? Like ships at sea we meet and pass and exchange greeting — and then sail out again upon the lonely waters — nor can all the ships upon the sea ever make those waters other than a far-stretched loneliness. Far away we sail, meeting for a moment, and then dipping downward toward opposite horizons, and unplumbed seas roll between us. This is one of the conditions of life — keenly felt by some, less keenly by others — but in some degree even by the most thoughtless, and perhaps most keenly by those of whom we suspect it least.

Now with Elijah this loneliness has two forms: it is the loneliness of being misunderstood — and equally of misunderstanding. He has the consciousness of having acted rightly, nobly, heroically — and of having failed. He knows himself to possess the only true clue of life. Far from the false and fevered life of courts and cities, he has nourished his soul in strenuous simplicity of thought and righteousness of conduct. He would fain have all Israel in correspondence with his ideal. He is absolutely sure that the one path of national happiness is that to which he points, and he cannot understand that what is so obvious to him, should be so incomprehensible to others. Every man who aims at the reform of society has to endure this bitterness. The youth who tries to live a life of chivalry and purity in the office: the merchant who cares more for honour than for gain: the statesman who is determined to steer a straight course in opposition to the casuistries of party interest: the social reformer who has mastered the right principles of social betterment, and is determined to apply them — all feel this pain of being misunderstood. It amazes and hurts them beyond measure to find that the world not merely does not believe in their ideals, but believes still less in their own purity of aim. The higher they climb the deeper is the loneliness which encompasses them, and it is with a shock that they discover that few or none follow them, till at the foot of some last inaccessible summit, on which a desolate and unanswering serenity dwells, they fall and cry —"Lord, take away my life; what am I better than my fathers?"

But this loneliness is equally the loneliness of misunderstanding. Elijah completely underrates his own work and influence. He says that he alone serves the Lord — it is not true. There are seven thousand quiet and unknown souls who serve Him too, and who have not bowed to Baal. The influence of a man like Elijah travels in the atmosphere. His words are flashed by a sudden spiritual telepathy upon a thousand ears, of which he knows nothing. You can count heads, you can tabulate numbers, but you cannot reckon influences. The lifting of a hand, the breathing of a word, reports itself on waves of imperceptible vibration to the furthest stars, and can a moral influence like Elijah's fail to touch men? Here and there a man says to the speaker of a truth, or the writer of a book, *Sir, you have blessed me:* but how many have received the same message and the same blessing and said nothing? Is it not true that the men who have seemed to fail have often been the only men in a generation who have really succeeded? John Keats, dying young, poor, and derided in Rome, thought that he had failed, and said his name was written in water: we know that it was written in adamant, and that he ranks with the immortals. Robertson of Brighton, dying in the prime of manhood, after a relatively obscure and bitterly misunderstood ministry, seemed to have failed: we know to-day that his sermons have touched the very springs of modern life, and have affected the teaching of the pulpit as perhaps no others ever have. Years after the death of Robertson, a Brighton tradesman said that whenever he was tempted to any underhand trick or lying compromise in business, he went into the little room behind his shop, and looked at Robertson's portrait and then felt he could not do it. Can any man be said to have failed who can produce this feeling in another man? The fact is, truth and goodness never fail, and there is more truth and goodness in the world than we suppose. The best influences of a good man's life are never known to him: if they were he could not say, "I, even I only, am left a prophet of the Lord," for his ears would be filled with the march music of that innumerable army who throughout the world fear God and work righteousness, and are his faithful comrades and eternal brothers in arms.

Elijah was presently to learn this lesson, but before he learned it he was to pass through a great experience. At this point all that we see is this gaunt and tragic figure in the desert — the strong man weak, the hero unmanned, lonely with so vast a loneliness that his mouth is full of reproach, his heart of bitterness. What was that experience? In what way did he discover the cure of loneliness? God calls him forth to look upon a great and terrible sight, and through the symbols of that vision we may find our way to the cure, as Elijah did. Now the essence of this vision is that it is a series of proposed cures for loneliness, each of which fails, until we reach the last.

First of all, freedom is suggested as a cure for loneliness. As Elijah stands in the mouth of the cave, and looks out, a great and strong wind rises and rends the mountains: and this we may take as the symbol of freedom. The mighty wind that beats over land and sea breathes the very spirit of liberty. It calls to the lonely man, and says, "Come, share the liberty of my life: travel forth with me: go out on your world-wandering with me: and in the thrill of speed and movement all loneliness of soul will be charmed away." That cry rings through all the movements of our time. Men who are lonely because they cannot find God, because truth eludes them, because impracticable ideals torture them, are told to claim the freedom of the earth, and leave a diseased society to heal itself.

> The days are dark and cold, and the skies are gray
> and old,
> And the twice-breathed air blows damp:
> You have heard the beat of the off-shore wind,
> And the thresh of the deep sea rain,
> You have heard the song, how long, how long,
> Put out on the trail again.

And who that is not wholly deadened in heart does not sometimes thrill to the appeal? Why toil for a society that does not seek to understand you, and will not love you? Life is short, and the joy of life is shorter than life. In a few years the stiffness and rigidity of age will creep over thought and impulse, and the days will come when we say we have no pleasure in them. So the wind thunders by, and calls to the lonely man, and it is as though all the trumpets of liberty blew, and the hard task drops from the hands at the sound, and the man in the cave's mouth stretches forward, as though he would beat out his way into that primeval freedom where there is no quest of truth, no burden of duty, no torturing ideals — but one thought arrests him — *God is not in the wind.* Liberty without God, what cure is there in that for the soul of man? No, let the wind thunder past, until at last it dies away, far off in the hollows of the night — there is no cure here — *for God is not in the wind.*

This truth is clear and manifest enough, if we think of it, but how slow we are to learn it. For does it not all lie in this, that we cannot fly from ourselves? Merlin, as he wanders in the enchanted forest of the Arthurian legend, is free — in a sense, indeed: but in no real sense. And why? Because "he is crushed and haunted, and vexed for ever by dim, unappeasable shadows of doom — whispers of the inexpiable, the irretrievable, the gone, the lost, the harvest passed, the summer ended!" In other words, he is haunted by himself. No man ever yet found anything but sorrow in flying from a duty. Emigration is no cure for heartache. We have to live with ourselves, whatever stars shine over us, and the man who lives with a dishonoured self, lives with misery. No: such revolt as this is no gain. The man in the cave's mouth may well draw his mantle over his head and turn away, for God is not in the wind.

And after the wind there came an earthquake — of what is this the symbol? May it not stand for that violence of action, that whirl of things, which always attracts the lonely man and promises to cure his grief? The kingdoms of the earth are always being shaken, social edifices are falling, shocks and changes are running through the nations, and amid the confusion there is an endless opportunity for ambition. The earthquake is even now shaking the throne of Ahab, and why should not a man of Elijah's force and courage seize that throne? The shaking of the old kingdoms always gives a chance to the ambitious man: it is the opportunity of Napoleon, and on the ruins of the earthquake which overwhelmed Europe, he builds his power. And for us, in lesser measure, the same vision is set. We can give up troublesome ideals and live for self. Amid the crash of other people's fortunes we can seize the chance to make our own. We need not even be sordid or meanly ambitious: we may find our lure in the power that comes to ability, amid the shiftings and uncertainties of society. Again the man in the cave's mouth looks out, and sees the shock run along the hills and shatter them, and feels the vast vibration like a wave beneath his feet, that lifts him onward and outward to a great career of power, of pride, of fame, but once more the thought arrests him — *God is not in the earthquake.* Such a life might fill the heart with noise; never with peace. It might drown thought, it could not uplift it. It might drive loneliness away in its merely superficial forms, but it would leave the heart emptier, lonelier, more isolated than ever. The seismic wave subsides beneath his feet, and once more he draws his mantle over his brows, and says, No. Here also is no cure — *God is not in the earthquake.*

And *after the earthquake came a fire:* the storm followed, and the live lightning leapt from crag to crag, and the whole body of the heavens became a mass of flame and splendour. It was the spectacle of the greatness and grandeur of Nature. Who is Elijah, who and what is any man in the presence of that elemental majesty? How small and vain all our poor earthly contentions seem when the silence of the stars, the diapason of the thunder, the rush of the tempest fills our imagination! We ask our little questions but there is no reply; there is even the suspicion of ghostly laughter in that hollow whisper of the night, of contempt in that tremendous voice of the thunder. In that vast battle of the heavens, man and all his petty armaments are overwhelmed; Ahab and Elijah are forgotten, Baal and Jezebel are words without significance. And this also we have felt, and to the man of grieved and lonely heart, Nature is proposed to-day, as she has always been, as the great mother who alone can heal us. Yet when have we ever found it so? To the finer sense there is indeed a species of communion with Nature, but it is loneliness answering loneliness not healing it. Wordsworth, more than any other man, sought that communion and found it, but even with him the cure was only partial, but he tells us —

Me, this unchartered freedom tires,
I feel the weight of chance desires.

Byron sought it, when he fled from the devastating passions of London to the icy stillness of the Alps, but of him it is said —

No hush fell on him, where the might
Of snow-capped peaks in solitude
Taught greater souls serenity:
Ah, vain his flight who flees from good.
Until man from himself can fly
What ease comes to him in his flight?

If indeed Nature can cure the lonely heart, why was not Elijah cured, for in the desert he was alone with Nature in its wildest forms of beauty and desolation? Yet can we not fancy this man once more bending forth from the cave's mouth, thrilled and dazzled by the splendour of the storm, thinking within himself that here in this cave he may find a rest — that here he can dwell content and secure in the lap of Nature, and share her calm, and rejoice in her terrors, and leave Ahab and all the vain world forevermore alone? But again the thought arrests him — *God is not in the storm.* No, man wants something more than beauty and magnificence to fill his heart. He needs duties, love, truth — the certainty and the manifestation of God; and the heavens burn in yet more blinding splendour, and the thunder rolls in yet nearer magnificence — *but God is not in the fire!*

And then at last a thing strange and wonderful happened — the wind, the earthquake, the thunder all pass, and a thrilling silence fills the desert. Earth and sky are hushed into deepest calm, exhausted by the passage of so much terror and confusion, and there is no sound save the faint breathing of the man in the cave's mouth, who still gazes into the void. *And after the fire came a still, small voice* — and at that voice the soul of the man thrilled, for it was the voice of God. "What doest thou here, Elijah?" It was the voice of rebuke, and of just rebuke. It is not here that loneliness can be cured — God is the one cure for the lonely heart. Liberty, ambition, beauty, take them all — for all are worthless. God made man for Himself, and for man there is no rest till he finds rest in God. So said St. Augustine many centuries ago; and, in our own day, has not Thomas Carlyle, who like Elijah sought comfort in the wind, and the earthquake, and the fire, also told us in his last letters, that the longer he lived, the more his heart went out to the truth of that saying he learned as a boy in the Scotch Catechism — "What is the chief duty of man? It is to know God and to enjoy Him forever." A voice — it is only one who lives who can speak — and Nature is dead and dumb. A still voice — it comes from the calm of eternity and breathes tranquillity through the soul. A small voice — no thunder this, but a voice demanding silence in the soul — the hearing ear, the attentive heart —

> So through the thunder comes a human voice
> Saying, O heart I made, a heart beats here,
> Face, my hands fashioned, see it in myself,
> Thou hast no power, nor may conceive of mine,
> But love I gave thee, with myself to love,
> And thou must love me who have died for thee!

And at that voice Elijah goes forth from the cave, and his heart is healed — for who can be lonely when God talks with him, or call himself forsaken when God consoles him?

I speak especially to lonely men and women, to those who cannot speak their deepest thoughts, or have none to whom they dare confide them; to those on whom the loneliness of great cities themselves weighs like a cloud, or those who know the loneliness of the house where death has been, or where poverty abides — and I point you to the one cure. Who can be lonely if Christ indeed be in the world, a spiritual comforter forevermore? Who can be uncomraded when the hospitable heart of God stands open to him? "I am alone, yet not alone," said Christ, for He dwelt in God and God in Him. Nor are these mere echoes of vague and transcendental truths. Upon the lips of the sick, of the life-long martyrs who know the pain without the palm, of the men and women who lie through long hours in solitary rooms, with their life slowly draining from them, how often have I heard the words —"Alone, ah! yes sir — but never lonely — for Christ is with me all the time!" How often have I seen upon the faces of the aged and the dying that quiet light, as though they saw a glory I could not perceive, and heard a voice inaudible to me. We also may find that joy of theirs, for we may hear the still, small voice. Lonely life must always be for many of us, and to others of us whose lives are crowded now, lonely hours come later, when the buoyancy of impulse and the power of executing purpose ebbs, when the house is empty and the children we have loved and toiled for are scattered through the earth; and for all of us there must needs come that last loneliness of death. But even then there is a voice that says, "I am with you alway," and it has been in the power of myriads of men and women to reply in that solemn hour, "Yea will I not fear." This is our hope, in God. This is our source of strength, that we live unto God, and not unto man. This is our final peace and satisfaction, that he who lives in God shares a fellowship with the eternal, which conquers the monotonies and depressions of time, and finds its fruition in the life that lasts when all earthly things have passed away. O tired and lonely heart, turn away from all vain dreams of cure in change of earthly state; bow thyself in the deep hush of this hour of prayer, and you shall hear the still, Divine voice which says, "My peace I give unto you, not as the world gives, give I unto you. Be of good cheer, I have overcome the world."

THE GREATNESS OF MEN SEEN IN HUMAN PROGRESS

VIII

THE GREATNESS OF MEN SEEN IN HUMAN PROGRESS

"We have not wrought any deliverance in the earth; neither have the inhabitants of the world fallen."—Isaiah xxvi. 18.

THIS passage may be taken as a pathetic and half ironical statement of the futility of human life. It is equivalent to saying "we expected to do great things with our life, and we have not done them," and this is a lamentable but common confession among men. Few men accomplish the dream of their youth, and in proportion as these dreams are high and vast, the probability of accomplishment becomes more and more remote. It is a catholic experience in life to discover that as we grow older hope takes a more sober hue, and ambitions moderate themselves; the conquest that once seemed so easy appears more and more difficult; the prize that seemed within our grasp eludes us, and recedes further from us with each narrowing period of life. Beyond all this, there are sudden checks which happen in prosperous careers; inexplicable misfortunes, reverses, and defeats; strange. and as it seems to us, unjust operations of blind circumstance, which suddenly deprive us of the triumph which we have had every reason to anticipate. All men know something of these experiences before they are done with life, and they are the bitterest experiences that man can know. Some take them with cynical indifference, some with philosophic acquiescence in the strange ways of destiny, some with vociferous complaint; but behind all our moods there exists a poignant sense of the futility of life, a sense of the uselessness and even the irony of high purposes in a world like this. It is this feeling that finds its expression in the saying of this ancient Hebrew poet—"We have not wrought any deliverance in the earth."

But a moment's thought will show you that much more than this lies behind this saying. It is in reality not the exposition of the humiliation of man, but of his undying greatness. For why should man expect to work any deliverance in the earth? For whom is that deliverance to be wrought? Whence comes the instinct which prompts the aim of such deliverance? What other creature is there capable of such an aspiration? We know of none. So far as we can see, man alone knows the torture of such a thought, and man alone is capable of that combined and corporate activity, which suggests to him the great hope expressed in the word *deliverance*. And this fact about man has been noted and commented upon from the very first. Three great allegories stand in the background of all human thought, each one of which helps to express man's sense of his own importance in the universe. The Eden-story of Genesis represents man as becoming as the gods, by his knowledge of good and evil; that is to say by his power of moral choice, which makes his life an undying struggle in pursuit of moral aims. The Greek story of man stealing the fire of the gods, is but a variation of the same allegory — the sublime statement of man's power to scale the heavens. And again, the story of Prometheus chained to the rock, eternally agonised, but eternally unconquered by his agony, is the allegory of man's power to resist and overcome the direst hostility of fate and circumstance. Combine these thoughts into one truth, and you have this result: that man feels himself placed upon the earth as the agent of divine purposes that go beyond himself. He feels himself ordained and predestined to work out some deliverance for himself and others — intellectual, moral, spiritual, and social deliverance; and his true life lies in this, and nothing else. "No one is unhappy at not being a King except a dethroned King," says Pascal, or we may add, who feels himself to be capable of Kingship: and no one mourns that he has wrought no deliverance in the earth, except a creature who realizes that it was his duty, his privilege, and the very mission of his life to accomplish such a deliverance. Thus, then, so far from being a melancholy statement of the futility of human life, this passage is the very opposite: it is the statement of the greatness of man as seen in human progress.

First of all, let us look at this statement of the greatness of man. It is manifest that if it be true, it is the most important of all statements, because it is capable of the most far-reaching consequences on human character and destiny. Conceive to yourself two children born into the world, one of whom is told from his birth that he is a creature of no importance: the other of whom is daily stimulated and encouraged by the great records of human achievement, and is told to emulate them. Conceive further two conditions of society, in one of which it is impressed on men that human existence is a malady and a misfortune, in the other of which, the glory, the joy, and the triumph of living are constantly expressed. Conceive yet again, two religions: the one teaching the utter misery of existence, the other teaching that man is but a little lower than the angels, and the express and permanent image of the unseen God who rules the universe. No one needs to be told what the effect these differing conceptions will be upon the human mind. There are families which through long centuries have bred heroic and chivalrous men and women, because self-reverence, honour and heroism were traditions in them. There are countries that have nourished great races because from father to son through many generations great and dignified ideals of religion and moral responsibility have been handed down untarnished. But the Bayard of perfect courtesy and chivalry rarely comes to growth in the foul slums of great cities where everything expresses the meanness of existence: the great deeds of human progress are never found among nations governed by pessimistic ideals of philosophy and religion. So then we see that what a man becomes depends largely on the estimate he forms of himself. The sense of human greatness makes men great: the sense of human littleness lessens them, and at last not only dwarfs but distorts and deforms them. He who preaches the total and unalleviated depravity of human nature not merely utters a psychological absurdity, but perpetrates a crime upon society, and an outrage on the cause of morals. And such a dogma receives no support from the religion of the Bible, which above all things states the dignity of man, his greatness, and his possibilities of growing greatness, likening him to God whose offspring he is, and bidding him be perfect even as the Father in heaven is perfect. The Bible may be right or wrong in such magnificent assertions — that is not in discussion with us for the moment — but no one can doubt that it does state from first to last, in matchless splendour of phrase and with unqualified boldness of language, the truth that man is great; and only a creature conscious of his greatness could utter the sublime lament that he had wrought no deliverance in the earth.

But is the Bible mistaken in these assertions, and is this passage after all but another example of that exalted egotism of which man has always been absurdly capable?

There are certainly three directions in which the least competent observer may discover reasons to doubt this assertion of the greatness of man. Compare man with physical nature, for example, and at first sight it is the insignificance and not the greatness of man that is apparent. But it is only at first sight. Mountains are great, but man can pierce them: seas are great, but man can traverse them: the storm-cloud is great, but man can pluck from its bosom the winged fire on which thoughts travel round the world. The whole thing is a fallacy, and the key to the fallacy is that magnitude is not greatness. What is mere bulk in comparison with thought and consciousness? What is the utmost majesty of matter in comparison with the magnificence of that spirit which gives to a man wisdom and understanding? We feel the Alps that tower above the St. Gothard to be great, but it is only in the sense of magnitude; when we see the engine man has fashioned slowly climbing up the mountain side, impelled by a mere handful of fire within its iron entrails; when we see it vanish in the bowels of the earth, and presently come forth again, having threaded with resistless energy and in complete triumph and security, the very roots of the everlasting hills — then we feel that we are in the presence of quite another sort of greatness — a greatness not of magnitude but of power. And as a matter of plainest fact the physical universe has no greatness except as it exists in the human mind. Pascal put the truth long since when he said, " If the universe were to fall and crush me, I should be greater than the universe, for I should be conscious of defeat, and it would be unconscious of victory." It is easy enough I grant to feel our insignificance as compared with nature, but the feeling is irrational, and quite illusory. Do not be misled by what poets have to say on such a theme. Do not mistake their expression of a natural emotion for the statement of a fact. God is great, and man is great, but elsewhere there is no greatness — and it is the authentic miracle and dignity of man as a creature truly God-like that we most need to learn if we are to live in such a way as to work out any deliverance upon the earth.

We may find reason to doubt the greatness of man, again, when we compare the total action of man with his aspiration. The aspiration is magnificent, but what of its fruit? Who attains a tenth part of that which he desires to attain: with whom is the efficiency of the accomplished action equal to the impulse that wrought it? Yes: but that very aspiration itself is a sort of greatness. To will great things is only less great than to accomplish them. The triumph of the individual man lies not only in that which he does, but in the great schemes and hopes which he desired to perfect, and which he bequeaths to the race, as the leaven of moral energy which shall work to its fulfilment long after he is dead.

And, in the third place, the greatness of man appears an empty phrase, when we compare man with himself. Think of the ineffectual lives that are lived upon the earth. Think of the lives distinguished by no lofty ideals, and abounding in every mean variety of motive. Think of the useless or noxious lives that spoil society: the hosts of men who never know a higher impulse than self-interest: the youths who spend the freshness of their manhood in idle sport and empty pleasure: the women who have no view of things outside the cloistered walls of decent domesticity — the people, for whom such terms as society, the commonwealth, the community, the nation, the world, have not the least significance, and for whom this passage is in consequence the merest tinkling of a cymbal, and a meaningless exuberance of rhetoric. But it is precisely at this point that the higher message of the text discloses itself. Let the individual be what he will, there is a general movement in society which makes for progress. *You* may not seek to work out any deliverance in the earth, but there are those who do so seek. A ceaseless impulse runs through men, coming we know not whither, and it impels them forward, ever forward. In spite of human apathy laws do get mended, reforms are accomplished, programmes once discredited transform themselves to facts. Some stand aloof, some are swept onward by the tide: but the tide never ebbs. Some smile in ignorant scorn, as doubtless the Swiss peasants did, when the first company of Engineers attacked the frowning bastions of the St. Gothard: but the day comes when the engine climbs the heights, and the iron rails bind two separated lands together; and then the dullest know that something has happened by which the whole world reaps benefit. You may not see the greatness of man as he stands against the immutable magnificence of nature: you may not see it in the individual or in yourself, but you do see it in human progress, and he who has once seen that vision will not be content to die until he has contributed his mite of energy to the sum of "things forever working," and has helped to work some deliverance in the earth.

And now let us go a little further and ask what is Progress? Progress is not wealth, though it is a common assumption that when you have proved a nation to be richer by the passage of the years you have proved that it has progressed. Progress is not personal success in life, though for multitudes that is the only meaning which the word conveys. There is such a thing, as Carlyle ironically reminded us, as progress downward. No: we must seek a higher and completer definition of the word — and we find it in this passage — Progress is deliverance. When a nation is delivered from ignorance by the universal establishment of free or cheap education — that is progress. When a nation is delivered from the tyranny of Kings, and the worse tyranny of landed and hereditary oligarchies — that is progress. When children are delivered from the pressure of inhuman factory laws: when fair wages and wise consideration bind masters and men together in honourable intercourse and self-respecting friendship: when churches are delivered from their theological animosities and arrogant assumptions, and are united in common effort for the common good; when men of all ranks have a common reverence for just ideals of government, and none are for a party and all are for the state: when virtue thrives, and vice is everywhere discredited, and the causes that produce vice are everywhere diminished by social service, wise statesmanship, and loyal love of good — that is progress. And every age presents some special opportunity of progress. Luther, Cromwell, Wesley, Lincoln — each is a name that tells its own tale of progress. Resolve progress into its elements, and what is it then but this: a long series of deliverances by which society grows freer, purer, and stronger: battles that begin obscurely in the convictions of single men, and end by becoming vast campaigns conducted by entire nations: struggles to attain, at first on the part of the enlightened few, but later on communicating their passion and their fervour to multitudes; deliverance upon deliverance, and each a stepping stone by which the world advances to its golden age. Yes: that is progress: that and nothing else. To live thus is indeed to prove that man can be great. Progress thus interpreted is indeed a Divine thing — the witness of God's government as of man's greatness. And to the man who once feels the fervour of this vision no disaster can be so great, no lamentation so poignant, as to be forced into confession as he leaves the world behind him, "Alas, I have misinterpreted the meaning of life, I have spent my money for that which is not bread, I have bartered my life for that which satisfieth not, I have wrought no deliverance in the earth!"

And of all certain things this is perhaps the most certain: that ideals such as these have most fascination for us when we are young, most power to move us, and are most likely to become permanent forces in our life. We believe in man then: we believe in the regeneration of society, and the promise of a golden age. You will find that in almost every case of a brave spirit struggling for the redemption of society from some form of deadly intellectual error, of political injustice or religious bondage, the struggle began early, in the days of youth. Later on belief in man becomes more difficult, and our sense of the obstacles to human progress is apt to become overwhelming. And therefore I say that this subject is of incomparable and paramount importance to youth. Do you really desire to work out any deliverance upon the earth? Have you felt the passion of the ideal? Do you hear the trumpet of the great campaign calling, and hear it with an eager heart? Choose ye, this day then, whom ye will serve, God or mammon. Remember now thy Creator, and the purpose for which thou wert created, in the days of thy youth. Set your hand to the plough of progress while its strength is yet undiminished, before the days come when desire shall fail. The day of diminished physical strength comes to all, but the day of diminished spiritual power need never come. For those who take life in a great spirit, for those who live for great purposes, that day never does come: they go from strength to strength: they advance from nebulous enthusiasm to settled hope: and from their lips the melancholy cry is never wrung — We have not wrought any deliverance on the earth.

And to this one other thing may be added, that the deliverance of man can only come by man. It would have been easy for the Creator so to have created man that at a glance and without effort he might have read the secret of the stars, and the solution of the baffling problems written in the great stone book of Nature. But that was not God's will: and we ourselves can see some reason for it. We see that the mind of man has been indefinitely developed by its pursuit of science, and that had the difficulties been less, the gain to intellectual growth would have been less also. And in the same way God does not solve for us by some miraculous interference the moral and social problems of the earth. We have to work out the earth's deliverance, and in doing so we work out our redemption. We have to do it: you and I: the least as well as the greatest of us. We can and do, each of us, help or hinder the cause of human progress. We all know how coral reefs are built. We know that every tiny cell in the growing reef is a tiny life that exhausts itself in fulfilling the mystic architecture of the reef, and when at last the completed reef rises from the blue abyss of water, and becomes an island on which the palm trees spring, and men find a habitation and a home, it is the aggregate effort of myriads upon myriads of minute creatures that triumphs there. So progress is the aggregation of multitudinous human effort. Every life lived rightly, every struggle of the individual after righteousness and justice, every humble effort of the humblest man or woman to make the world a better world, is a contribution to the scheme of things which the Master Architect has designed as the crown of human existence; and so it comes to pass that the humblest man may know before he dies that he has helped to work out some Divine deliverance on the earth.

And so two lives stand clear before us, and two endings to life, each of which is possible to each of us. There is the life of the man delivered from himself: from inordinate ambition, vain pleasure, self-ease, and sensual hope: the life that gives itself a ransom for many, and dedicates itself to the great crusades of moral progress, and this is the Christian life. Such a man knows well what the lines mean —

> He only lives the world's life
> Who hath renounced his own.

He knows also what the saying means —

> Renounce joy for thy fellow's sake
> That's a joy beyond joy.

And the end of such a life is triumph. All that he desired is not accomplished: but enough is done to assure him that right is triumphing, and that truth prevails: and so his final word is heroic — it is the farewell of the happy warrior —" I have fought the good fight, I have finished my course with joy."

The other life begins and ends within itself. It contributes nothing to the public good, perhaps it hinders it. It is indifferent to all the struggles of the race: it scorns the enthusiasm of great men: it rises up to eat, it lies down to sleep — it sees the troops of freedom march to battle, it hears far off the trumpets blow, but it sits enchanted in its web of sloth, in its grossness of ignoble ease, and hearing it hears not, and seeing it does not understand. If at last it does see itself aright, it wakes only to discover the chances of a manful life for ever lost, and to bewail itself in the melancholy cry, " I have wrought no deliverance in the earth." Those two lives in all their issues stand before each of us, and it is for us to choose which life shall be ours. Up, up, thou eager heart of youth, and hear the voice that calls thee! Up thou idle one and work while it is called to-day, before the night cometh when thou canst not work! The torn flag of freedom floats upon the gale: the chivalry of Christ sweeps on to the endless Armageddon: your land, your motherland is calling you to help her. A thousand schemes of progress are yet unfulfilled, a thousand hopes stand disinherited, a thousand thousand voices of the poor and the oppressed call for the coming of the champion and deliverer. Up, and follow the captain of salvation; deliver the oppressed, bind up the broken-hearted, bring liberty to the captive; and know this, that they that "be wise shall shine as the brightness of the firmament, and they that turn many to righteousness as the stars for ever and ever."

THE EXPLOITS OF FAITH

IX

THE EXPLOITS OF FAITH

"But the people that do know their God shall be strong, and do exploits."— Dan. xi. 32.

MANY things about the Book of Daniel are difficult and disputed, but one thing is tolerably clear, and this gives us the clue to the book — it was undoubtedly written for the encouragement of Jewish patriotism. No nation was ever so intensely patriotic as the Jewish, because none had so powerful an historic sense. The greatest hymns of the nation were glowing recapitulations of national history — the promise to Abraham, the deliverance from Egypt, the long story of the wilderness and the promised land. The most solemn acts of public worship were vitally connected with national history, and when the Jew of to-day, standing an alien in the strange world of London, begins a discourse upon the Feast of Tabernacles, as I once heard for myself, with the sentence —"Three thousand five hundred years ago to-day"— he strikes the chord of patriotism that survives all the change of empire and civilization, and the vicissitudes of time. But Jewish patriotism differs from every other form of patriotism in the fact that it is dominated completely by the sense of God. It recognises not only its own part in history, but God working through all events His indisputable and sovereign will. It reads past, present, and future, not in the light of the human only, but of the Divine. And thus Daniel expresses all that is noblest in this patriotism, when he links God with, or rather enthrones God *in* the centre of all Jewish heroism, by saying "The people that know God shall be strong, and do exploits."

In all human history it would be hard to find any figure so pathetic and sublime as the Jew. He has been the prey of all nations and their master, their spoil and their spoliator. He has been flung down into an unutterable depth of infamy, but the infamy has constantly recoiled upon his persecutors. His lot has been made bitter by every species of wrong, cruelty, and inhumanity, but he has survived them, and like the great disowned Prophet of his nation has been constantly crucified, only to rise again upon the third day. In the utmost darkness he has found a light to guide him, and amid the most terrible of deprivations a hope to console and support him. He stands amid new nations and civilizations to-day, himself unchanged — the wonder and the enigma of the world. He has survived the Roman and the Greek, and in turn he may survive the Teuton and the Anglo-Saxon. If we can fancy any human creature standing on the ruins of Westminster bridge and surveying the desolation that was once called London, it will not be Lord Macaulay's mythical New Zealander — it will be a Jew. In the presence of this strange race all the people of modern Europe are but children just out of school; for the Jew had a literature and a philosophy, when our forefathers were barbarians and worshipped blocks of wood and stone. And as one surveys that literature and philosophy; as one endeavours to arrive at the secret hidden in all this long, chequered, pathetic and sublime history, one fact continually emerges: the greatest periods of the nation coincide with the periods when the sense of religion was strongest among the people: the most terrible downfalls and dispersions with the loss of that religious sense. It is not merely a philosophic truth, therefore, which is stated in this passage, it is an historic fact, for the Jew has been strong and done exploits because he has known his God.

The theme which this passage suggests then is the certainty of God as the secret of noble human achievement. Let me, in the first place, make three preliminary observations. The first is that *the total effect of modern science has been to make the existence of God an absolute necessity of human reason.* Fifty years ago such a result was not anticipated, and at a much more recent date it was generally assumed that the final effect of science would be the destruction of religion. But as the great conjectures and discoveries of science have followed one another in their startling sequences, it has more and more been felt that the last step of science leaves us kneeling before the altar which is dedicated to the unknown God. Science has told us much about the functions of life, and the infinitely delicate and wonderful contrivances by which these functions are discharged, but it has failed utterly to tell us what life is and to explain its origin. It has explained the brain, but it has not told us how poetry, imagination, and thought come into existence. It has gone through the house of life, unlocking every door, but before one door which conceals what religious men call the chamber of the soul it has paused, confessing inadequacy and defeat. It has traversed every road of space, only to find itself finally face to face with the inscrutable and mysterious Power that inhabits eternity, and fills all things. Natural Law — yes, it has codified that with marvellous skill and patience, but it has also been forced to confess some Intelligence which is at once the controller and inventor of natural law. And this all true men of science have long ago admitted. Materialism has had its day, and its power is already gone. The intelligent man can no longer content himself within limits so narrow and confined. He would never have tried to do so, if he had more closely observed the spirit of his masters, for Darwin himself adopts as a motto for his famous "*Origin of Species*" the saying of Bishop Butler, that the only "distinct meaning of the word natural is stated, fixed, and settled: and that it as much requires an intelligent agent to effect anything statedly, fixedly, regularly — that is naturally — as to effect it for once only — or supernaturally." And that, I need not tell you, is the confession of science that without God the universe is inexplicable.

The second observation I make is that *the morality of man is a guarantee of the moral nature of God.* Granted a Creator, it is a thing incredible that the creature should be greater than the Creator, for the river cannot rise higher than its source. Suppose that at the beginning of the Ten Commandments there were no preface, declaring that "God spake all these words and said": suppose that man had evolved entirely out of his own conscience the commandments not to kill, not to steal, not to covet, not to worship graven images and so forth; even then you would not be rid of God. For if man is the creature, and somewhere there exists a Creator, it follows, does it not, that the creature cannot reach a height of moral thought impossible to the Creator? If man feels that lying, adultery, and murder are wrong, we may be sure of it that there is some final and supreme authority which also judges these things as wrong. Thus the strongest witness to a moral God lies in the moral nature of man. Man has a right to say as John Stuart Mill said, "I will call no Being good, who is not what I mean when I apply that epithet to my fellow creatures, and if such a Being can sentence me to Hell for not so calling him, to Hell I will go." That is what man says as he stands before the silent altars of the invisible: he says there what he has said before the meaner tribunals of earth, "Here I take my stand, I can do no other." Whatever is moral in man exists in an infinite perfection in God: whatever is lovely, in a higher loveliness: whatever is pure in a loftier purity, and thus a man knows God by his knowledge of himself.

The third observation is, that the *ultimate meaning and the very essence of Christianity, is the revelation it gives us of man's capacity for God.* It does this not so much by the statement of a philosophic truth as by a practical and living illustration — the Person of Jesus Christ. It shows us a man, and says that if God lived upon this earth, His life would be precisely what the life of this man was. It shows us this man under every variety of circumstance: poor, despised, rejected: praised, flattered, hated: coming into awful collision with evil, not only in the deliberate conflict of the desert, but in the city, and in the daily conduct of life: following truth to His own destruction, loving His fellow men as no creature ever loved, consoled under every difficulty by the certainty of an invisible world of spirit more real and enduring than the actual world of the senses, going finally to His martyrdom with a sense of triumph — and it says, "Thus God would have done, had God been man": and again, "This was God, so revealed that all men may know Him": and yet again, "Even thus God may live in every man." The capacity for God — the power of the human soul to receive God into itself, the power of the humblest man to live as God would have lived, had God lived this life — that is the supreme revelation of Christianity, and those that thus know God shall be strong and do exploits.

And now let us turn once more to this suggestive saying. If these things are true, then they are the greatest of all truths. It may occur to some of you to complain that this theme is purely academic, and to ask what relation has abstract truth to human action? That is the question which is answered in this text. We all dwell in two worlds — the world of thought, and the world of conduct. No man dwells exclusively in either the one or the other. The thinker is not only a thinker, the doer is not only a doer. Both are engaged in one supreme occupation, which is the conduct of life, and life cannot be conducted except upon some acknowledged principles. In other words, you must have wise and right thoughts, if you are to live a wise and right life. It is the merest folly to say "It does not much matter what I think if I act rightly," because action is thought in motion, and what a man thinks he will inevitably do and be. And this is the plain meaning of this saying; what it amounts to is that the secret of all national life, all individual life, and all human heroism is found in religion — or in other words, is what nations and men think about God.

The *secret of all national life lies in national religion* — take that proposition first. Let me endeavour to put it not as an abstract truth, but by way of concrete fact. Suppose a man should leave the shores of England and go upon a pilgrimage to explore the unknown regions of the East. The first land that he would see would be the shores of Spain, and the rock of Gibraltar, and there at once the problems of national religion would salute him. He would look through the history of Spain, and he would discover that all the great episodes of its history were dominated by some religious idea. He would remember the reign of the Moors and their expulsion, the history of the Spanish Jews and their downfall, the Armada and its fate, and he would need no one to tell him that the greatest periods of Spanish history precisely coincided with the periods when the witness of God was strongest in the nation. He would touch upon the shores of Italy, and he would remember how a Jewish fugitive named Paul had landed there nineteen centuries ago, had preached his Gospel, and how that Gospel had spread, till the whole face of the world was altered by it. He would touch at Egypt, and there he would see the memorials of a splendid and mysterious religion, a religion that had its symbols of the Trinity, of incarnation and redemption, of resurrection and immortal life, thousands of years before Christ was born in Bethlehem. He would sail onward down the Red Sea, and all the history of Israel would unfold its panorama to the mental eye; he would come to India, and a thousand stately temples would witness to the sense of religion which has dominated the three hundred millions of that land of wonders through the long centuries. Thus the thought of God would pursue him to whatever land he went, and he would be unable to escape it. At many points these various systems of religion would differ, but he would see that men acted as if each were true, and that each was the offspring of the sense of God in man. He would find that religious ideas and hopes had entwined themselves with the laws, the customs, and the literature of these lands, and as he surveyed the customs of these diverse lands and peoples he would discover that the greatest movements in each national life had been religious movements. He would return to England and the same lesson would meet him in his own history. He would read of Lollards, Reformers, Covenanters, Puritans; he would read a thousand stories of heroic struggle out of which the strong tree of modern civilisation and liberty drew its strength; he would see vast political issues constantly springing out of the triumph of religious ideas. And everywhere one lesson — the people who knew their God were strong and did exploits, and in proportion to the power of religion over the national mind, was the greatness of the nation, and the height to which it attained in the scale of nations.

Again: *The Secret of the intellectual life of men reveals the same lesson.* For modern men some half a dozen names stand supreme as recording the greatest height to which intellect has attained. When we have mentioned Newton, Bacon, Shakespeare, Milton, Dante, Goethe, we have counted the brightest stars in the firmament of intellect. Turn to their teachings, and you will find at once that the keynote of each life was faith in God. Erase God from the writings of Shakespeare, Milton, or Dante, and they crumble into utter incoherence. Ask Bacon and Newton on what their whole philosophy is based, and they will answer without an instant's hesitation, "On God, the Primal cause, the Primal morality, the Primal goodness: the Light of lights, the Lord of lords, the King of kings!" Turn to Goethe, the most pagan of moderns, and you will hear him telling you in his old age that he trusts that he shall never be so weak as to lose his conviction in personal immortality. And if you come to modern times, the lesson is the same. All that we call poetry springs from man's conscious sense of God. The human mind can soar in one direction only, and that is upward. Could either Tennyson or Browning have been the great poets and teachers they were, had they not been permeated by the sense of God? Could even a Matthew Arnold have written as he did if there had not been under all his intellectual negations a solid substructure of inherited religious conviction? No: the history of the human mind is one long and invariable testimony to this truth, that the men who know their God, these are they that are strong and accomplish the magnificent exploits of genius.

Again: *turn to the story of human heroism* as it is written in the record both of men and nations, and it is not possible to mistake the enormous influence of religious belief on human conduct. Where is your hero who has not found the sanction of his heroism, and its vital impulse, in the sense of his relation to God? The fact is that atheism withers the heart, and is destructive of all those large and generous passions that make the hero. From the day when Stephen looked with dying eyes in the blue depths of the Syrian sky, and saw the heavens opened, and Jesus standing at the right hand of God — from that day and long before it — man has always encouraged himself in the great sacrificial exploits of heroism by the conviction that they are a duty which he owes to God as well as to man: and owes to man simply because he recognises his responsibility to God. We may say what we like about atheism but we cannot reason away the fact that it belittles human nature, and destroys its capacity for heroism. It means something — it means far more than we suppose — that a Socrates finds the secret of courage in the sense that he obeys a divine intuition which he calls his "dæmon," that a Joan of Arc hears "The voices" calling her to the thorny way of martyrdom — that a Nelson dies thanking God for his great opportunity of doing his duty. Teach a man that there is a higher voice than man's which he is capable of obeying — that he is surrounded by an unseen cloud of spirit witnesses, that heaven applauds him, that heaven stretches forth a starry crown for him, and that his dying may be but the birth-throe of a larger life — teach him that, and he can be a Hero. Teach a nation that, and a nation can be heroic. Then you have the sublime constancy of Vaudois peasants under every species of torture, and you have the revolt of the Netherlands which breathes into a little harried nation such a spirit of indomitable courage that it can oppose, and finally defeat, the malice of the greatest military power in Europe. They were strong, these Vaudois martyrs, these Piedmontese peasants, these plain Dutch burghers — they were strong and did exploits because they knew their God. They committed their souls to God in flame, and feared not what man could do unto them. They were conscious of invisible hosts that marched with them, and of an invisible Captain whose word like a trumpet stirred their hearts. They could die, but could not lie, they could be tortured and not accept the traitor's infamous deliverance. And from first to last in the long and splendid record of human heroism the story is the same; the heroic exploits of the world are the exploits of faith, and the greatness of man has always been nourished by the sense of a Power beyond and above the world, whose he was, and whom he served.

Nor need we turn only to departed history for the illustration of such experiences as these. Show me the greatest exploits of modern life, the most memorable episodes of human action, in which man is seen at his sublimest and his noblest. Where are these to be found in such gray days as ours, do you ask? The story of the Salvation Army is one, the life of Livingstone another, the daily history of missionaries in heathen lands and city slums, a third. Taken only as romance there is nothing in modern history more wonderful than the story of General Booth, no figure that moves upon a higher plane of heroism than Livingstone, as he passes into the abyss of the Dark Continent holding aloft his simple lamp of truth, no stories that display a loftier courage than the stories of modern missionaries — those daring adventurers of the Soul, who in a hundred lands have held not their lives dear unto them for the testimony of Jesus. Jesus — they never saw Him, but they have known His presence: they have heard His word, they have found God in Him, and this was the victory that overcame the world, even their faith. Jesus — He died nineteen hundred years ago in the flesh — yet is He alive for evermore, and they have known Him in the rapture of a fellowship that lifted them far above either the scorn or the fear of man. And so they did exploits, so they are doing them every day — men and women like ourselves who walk these dingy roads of life with crowns upon their heads, marching to the rhythm of a loftier music than the world supplies — they are strong and do exploits because they know their God.

It may perhaps be said, that great lives are not within the reach of most of us, and that, therefore, it is vain thus to speak as though the exceptional in human conduct could ever be the rule of the normal. But the value of great lives is that they set the measure of what all lives should aspire to be, and, therefore, we cannot speak too much of them. And, moreover, all greatness is relative, and the faith of Livingstone will make the life of any man noble, even though that life knows no sublime adventure, but is lived from first to last in complete obscurity, in humblest drudgery, and in conditions where it never can attract the eye of any single sympathetic or generous spectator. Or, again, it may be said, that such spiritual experiences as these — the experiences that make men great — do not happen to the common or the average man. Ah, but the common man also has his experiences — his high moments when God seems real and near to him, and will you remember that your "highest moments are your truest moments." Or it may be said, again, that to know God is a thing so difficult to man, so rare, so exceptional, and demands such a special temperament, that the ordinary man cannot attain to such convictions, and can only say in sadness, "Such knowledge is too wonderful for me, I cannot attain unto it." But we can all of us learn something of the Person of Christ — and religion is not the attainment of a great philosophic truth, but a love for Christ which makes us His disciples. God is truly revealed to us in Christ, and when we try to live just as Christ lived, then we live as God Himself has lived upon the earth, and multitudes of quite humble people have found that possible in every age by love and faith, and by the Gift and Power of the Holy Spirit. And so you, young man going into the city every day, you who have no wide sphere of influence, and earn your bread in some unknown bye-walk of this great crowded life around us — you can claim this text, and its promise is for you. You can practice what Jeremy Taylor called the great essential of holy living —"The practice of the presence of God." You can live as seeing Him who is invisible, and your whole life will put on a new dignity, and know a new and gracious peace for that vision. You will be strong and work exploits, living a life worth living, and that shall be memorable, if you will but open your heart to the knowledge of God, and live as ever in your great Taskmaster's eye. And amidst much that is mean in life, much that is sordid, much that is commonplace, you will live a life that is far from mean, or sordid, or commonplace, for you will learn to say with Russell Lowell in his great hymn of faith —

> God of our fathers, Thou who wast,
>   Art, and shall be —
> We who believe Life's bases rest,
> Beyond the probe of chemic test,
> Still, like our fathers, feel Thee near.

I do not grudge you the pleasures of youth: I do not suppose that you can each attain to philosophic insight and sobriety of thought: I do not imagine that it is within the compass of each of you to be what the greatest of men have been: but you can know your God, you can live in the steady sense of God's presence, and he who does this, be his mind never so limited in its range, and his life never so narrow in its opportunities, shall be strong, and shall do exploits.

THE CHANGED FORM, THE ONE CHRIST

X

THE CHANGED FORM, THE ONE CHRIST

"After that He appeared in another form unto two of them, as they walked, and went into the country."— Mark xvi. 12.

THIS is the bare record of one of the appearances of Christ to the disciples, fully told for us in the story of the journey to Emmaus which occurs in the last chapter of St. Luke's Gospel. That story is familiar to all of us. Two disciples, appalled by all that has occurred in Jerusalem, set out in the eventide for Emmaus convinced that the whole propaganda of Christianity is at an end, prepared to renounce its hopes and to take up once more the dreary tasks of a commonplace and unillumined life. As they walk and are sad they are overtaken by a stranger who talks with them in friendliest intercourse, accepts their hospitality, and is finally known to them as Jesus in the breaking of bread. Among the various incidents of the Resurrection this stands alone, if one may say so. Christ nowhere appears so simply human as in this episode of Emmaus. He is the friend and comrade: He wears no aspect of awe or majesty: He speaks no words that thrill the heart with a terror of the supernatural — only warm loving human words, which cause the hearts of these forlorn men to burn with passionate affection. This is made strikingly manifest in one circumstance: the women who see Him at the sepulchre are afraid, the disciples in the upper chamber, seeing a form of unearthly majesty outlined on the air, are terrified, and suppose that they have seen a spirit. But here there is simple gladness and no fear. Christ has appeared to them in another form — not as the supernatural, but the natural Jesus: not as the mysterious conqueror of the grave, but as the Human Friend and Leader.

The arresting thought of this passage lies in the phrase "another form." Does it not suggest that men see Christ with different eyes, and that Christianity itself appears to men in differing forms? Does it not suggest that religion allows full play for the varied idiosyncrasy of men, and that we must not expect every man to discern religious truth precisely as we ourselves discern it? And in this large allowance for the individual point of view, do we not find something thoroughly consonant with the known order of the world, and ought we not to learn a lesson in charity which we all need to learn? This is the theme which grows out of the text, and it is one eminently worth our careful and humble investigation.

I say, in the first place, that there is something in

this suggestion which is in thorough consonance with the known order of the world. Thus, for example, it is the plainest of all known facts, that no two men ever see any feature of the physical universe about us with quite identic vision. Two men look upon a sunset or a wide and distant view, but each sees the splendid pageant differently, and the kind of emotion which each feels manifests a wide, and possibly an irreconcilable, variation. Two men look upon a flower: but if the one man be Wordsworth, he sees in it thoughts that lie too deep for tears: and if the other man be a Peter Bell,

> In vain thro' every changeful year
> Does nature lead him as before:
> A primrose by the river's brim
> A yellow primrose is to him,
> And it is nothing more.

Two poets write of Nature: but where one sees law, the other sees love, and while for one the message of Nature is sombre and majestic immutability, for the other it is a kind of noble sympathy. Two artists go out to paint the same scene, but each sees something in it not manifest to the other, and when each has completed his picture you will find as wide a difference in the two pictures as you find in the two men. These are illustrations so simple and commonplace that they are familiar to the least observant, and they go to prove that we all see with different eyes.

Again, love always sees with different eyes. For the true lover there is something in the beloved that none but he can see — a beauty real to him, but perhaps wholly hidden from any one else, a grace and charm which thrill his heart but do not appeal so fully to another. This is one of the facts of human life, at once beautiful, pathetic, and astonishing. Few men marry beauty, but all think they do: they see an ideal image which to them is real, and years pass, and gray hairs come, and the bloom of youth perishes, but, where love is true and constant, all this havoc is not so much as noticed, and the old man beholds in the helpmeet of his life, not the worn and wasted form the world sees, but the wife of his youth, the bride that linked her hand with his before the altar. And in the same way, what woman is there who does not see a loveliness in her child which no one else sees? It is not always that a child is beautiful, but to the mother the plainest child is never less than beautiful: and often and often, my heart has been moved with the wonder and the sacredness of motherhood, when I have seen some woman following every movement of a quite unattractive child with wistful and adoring eyes, as though the child were the very image of a perfect beauty. How do we account for these things? Simply thus: these human creatures have appeared to those who love them in another form, and love has transfigured and transformed them.

Take another fact which brings us still nearer to our theme. The great object of all the greatest art of this world has been the person of Jesus Christ: but as you go through some great gallery filled with examples of Old Masters how astonishing is the divergence of interpretation which you find! The Christ of Michael Angelo, the Christ of Fra Angelico — a whole world of thought separates the two. For one painter the dominant image of Christ is an image of agony and shame, to him the Cross is the overwhelming and awful thing, and do what he will he cannot tear himself from the contemplation of that sublime majesty of woe, that speechless sorrow and expiring meekness. But to another painter the vital fact about Jesus is not His death but His perfect life with men: and so you have pictures of Christ asleep beneath the palm trees of Egypt, Christ in the temple with the money changers, Christ in the triumphant magnanimity of His dealings with sinful men and women. Michael Angelo sees Christ as the awful Judge of quick and dead: Fra Angelico as the dear human presence, moving among men in simple friendliness, and "feeding the faint divine in human hearts." Which was right? you say. It is not a question of right or wrong — each was right because each saw something that was true — each saw something that the other did not see — and Christ appeared to each in a different form.

It is but a step further to the perception of another truth, that in the whole history of Christ and His Church there has always been this divergence of view and interpretation, and this wide allowance for human idiosyncrasy. Take, for example, Christ's revelation of Himself in His earthly life. He speaks as an ascetic when He says that the life is more than meat: He acts with the most genial acceptance of the uses of life when He is the friend of publicans and sinners, and eats with them. He speaks as one for whom all the outward aspects of the world are meaningless when He talks of the Kingdom of God as within men: and again He speaks as one vividly awake to the significance of human events when He talks of the signs of the times, and declares the things that make for the peace of nations. He speaks as a non-combatant when He disclaims the use of the sword, and in yet another passage He proclaims that He comes to bring not peace, but a sword among men. He is at one moment the Good Shepherd, and the Lover of Souls: and at another the Judge, before whose face the wicked shall be burned up as tares of the field. He makes no effort to reconcile these varying aspects of Himself and His message. He does not create, and does not seek to create, a uniform impression on the minds of men. His words can be the severest of all words, and they can be the sweetest: to the hypocrite He is a sword, to the humble a sanctuary. And what does it all mean but this — that Christ recognised the infinite variations of human temperament, and He appeared in a different form to individual men, according to their power of apprehension, and their need of truth? And if this be true, it is equally true and indisputable, that the apostles, who were entrusted with the great task of interpreting Christ to the world, each saw Christ in a different form. It was natural that Paul, trained from childhood in Rabbinical lore, and a Pharisee of the Pharisees, should see Christ chiefly in His relation to ancient Jewish types and ceremonies, and should interpret all things in the light of His supreme and atoning sacrifice. But it was equally natural to John that he should shed upon the story of Christ the light of a sublime mysticism, and that James should see it in the light of practical duties. Nor did the apostles themselves profess any perfect coincidence of view. Peter boldly speaks of certain things in Paul's teaching which are hard to be understood, which the unlearned and ungodly wrest or dislocate out of right relation, to their own destruction. It is not too much to say that divergence of interpretation began with the first moment of the organised church, and through all ages these divergencies have gone on. Think of the endless growth of sects and churches — of Christianity as it was variously discerned by the Crusader, the Monk, and the Puritan: of the Christian of the Catacombs with his one simple and exquisite conception of the Shepherd with the lamb on

His shoulder, and the Christian of the mediæval ages, with his awful vision of Jesus as the King of Glory to whom approach was only possible through the softer virtues and gentle supplications of the Virgin Mother: think of religion as it is conceived in turn by Luther, Bunyan, and Wesley — by the High Churchman, the Quaker, and the Methodist: reflect not merely on the divergence of view involved in these conceptions of truth, but on the intense hostilities which they have provoked, the bitter feuds, the actual battles and cruel martyrdoms — and what have you to say to it all? There is but one thing that ought to be said — it is that Christ appeared to all these men in a different form. Each saw what he was capable of seeing, and each saw something that was vitally and therefore eternally true.

You will notice further that all the troubles of the Church have arisen from the attempt to enforce unity and identity of view. How significant is this simple statement of the Evangelist; "*He appeared in another form unto two of them: and they went and told it unto the residue: neither believed they them.*" No: they were willing enough to believe that their own revelation of Jesus was authentic — that the Jesus seen in the upper room, and the garden was real — but this pilgrim Jesus, talking with these two men on the road to Emmaus — this forsooth could only be hallucination. What they had seen and felt was true: what others had seen and felt was not credible:

so early do we find an illustration of the saying that orthodoxy is my doxy, and heterodoxy is everybody else's doxy. And this spirit, a spirit really of intolerant egoism and vanity, has been at work among men ever since; and it has caused more mischief, more disruption, more strife and clamour than any other score of causes you could name. It is a thing perfectly right and even noble in a man that he should say —"This is true, I pledge my life upon it!" but no man has the right to say "This *only* is true," because he ought to remember that something else may be true which it is not given him to discern. But the tendency of human nature is always to exalt a partial truth into the whole truth, and to label as falsehood any form of truth that does not commend or reveal itself to us. You can scarcely have a more pertinent illustration of this intolerance than in the case of Luther, who is eager to tear the whole Epistle of St. James out of the New Testament, because he is incapable of seeing how it shapes with the vital truth that man is saved not by works, but by grace and faith: and yet Luther himself was a great heretic, who had insisted upon his right of private interpretation of truth against the whole force of the Roman Church, and had asserted that Christ had appeared to him in another form, and that his own vision of Christ was to be respected and allowed. But the case is by no means unusual. You will constantly find that the man who claims liberty of judgment for himself is not prepared to extend that liberty to others. You will find that the man who in his youth is a heretic, contrives to elevate his heresy into orthodoxy by the time the period of middle life is reached, and that he who fought hard for tolerance in his manhood has become as intolerant as the worst inquisitor of Rome by the time old age is reached. If Luther was capable of recognising truth, surely St. James was not less capable, and had an even better opportunity: but no: this is the whole truth, says Luther, and he will not allow that Jesus had appeared to St. James in another form. In no other domain than theology do men dare to claim this arrogant right of infallibility. In politics, in science, in medicine, all thoughtful men are willing to admit that there is something to be said for the views of their antagonists. They recognise the falsehood of extremes, and the uncertainties of knowledge teach them diffidence and humility. But in theology, which is the most subtle and difficult of all sciences, depending less on intellectual deductions than individual intuition and experience — here, and here alone, men dare to speak with the accent of arrogant infallibility. And they do more: they are determined to force their views upon everybody. They will allow nothing for human idiosyncrasy. They libel, deride, defame, and excommunicate all who will not agree with them. They carry their creed upon the sword point, and are prepared to plunge whole nations into bloody war for the interpretation of a text, or even a phrase. In a word all that is most disgraceful in ecclesiastical history, all that has divided the Church and has dyed the garments of truth with the martyr's blood, may be traced to this one cause: men will not believe that Christ appears to their brothers in another form, and will not accept as truth, any statement of truth that differs from their own. *Neither believed they them:* it is the saddest sentence in the whole history of Christianity.

But from these general statements let us pass finally to those particular lessons which we all need to learn.

The first is that the revelation of Christ to the individual soul will always vary with the individual. The greatest miracle in all the world is the miracle of human individuality: that in a hundred million of men and women you will not find two exactly alike: two, who see things from precisely the same angle of vision; two, who know entire identity of thought and feeling. It is so that God has chosen to make His children; each man a world in himself, each with subtle variations of character and temperament, that distinguish him from all other human creatures. And thus it happens, that just as no two men see the world of nature as quite the same, so religion takes its own form for each. There is no one of us for whom all the doctrines of Christianity are equally important. There are moral and intellectual conditions which give sharpness and cogency to certain truths, and which invest some truths with a reality which we do not feel in relation to others. The fear of God is for one man the dominant note of all religion — the love of God for another: and there are changes of experience in ourselves which make one truth the whole truth to us in youth, and quite another truth the master-star that rules our maturer years. Christ appears to us in many forms — and if we compare our thoughts about Christ to-day with those fainter and more obscure perceptions that we had twenty years ago, we can mark a very wide change of view. And if we ourselves know variations of view, it is no cause for astonishment that other men see Christianity in quite a different light from ourselves. The one divine light has come to us and them, but it streams through a differing medium — yet it is the same light of life. The same Christ has appeared to the scholar in the upper room of learning, and to the humble disciple on the road of sorrow, but the revelation has been tempered to the need of each. Those also are disciples who do not see what we see: those also are Christians who are not of this fold. There are many voices of truth, but none without significance: there are many revelations of Christ to men, but He appears in a differing form.

The second lesson is that we should learn not to despise a revelation of truth which we ourselves do not need or comprehend. Think, for example, of the great multitude of souls who are numbered in the Roman Catholic communion. To us it may be that many of the predominant dogmas of the Roman Catholic faith are quite unintelligible or even profane. They mean nothing to us, and we cannot fancy ourselves, under any transformation or compulsion of circumstance accepting them. But it is certain that they mean much to these multitudes of souls. It is equally certain that there must be some element of vital truth behind them all, or they had never fastened themselves so firmly on the human mind and conscience through so many ages. We are prepared to admit that to the truly pious Catholic, Christ has appeared in another form; but the charity we practise we also claim. We demand that we shall not be called heretics by those whom we are prepared to call Christians. And in regard to the High Churchman we say the same thing. His view of truth is not ours: but we gladly admit that there is truth in his view and that Christ has appeared to him in another form. We give up nothing of our own convictions in such an admission: we ask him to give up none of his: but we do claim that we also have received our revelation of Christ, and that we also are His Church.

Think again of the nobler forms of pagan piety still extant in the world, and remember the exceeding breadth of the inspired statement that Christ is the light of every man who cometh into the world. The narrow-minded Christian is puzzled when he finds so much in the life of Buddha which closely resembles the life of Jesus. He is still more puzzled when he hears of natural religion among the heathen, of virtue, temperance, chastity, self-sacrifice, of reverence for sacred things, of sincere and ardent effort to live in the light of the highest known duty. But St. Paul found no difficulty in the presence of such facts. He admitted the existence of natural religion. And both in the Gospels and the Acts of the Apostles we have notable examples of noble-minded pagans who fasted, prayed, and gave alms, who cultivated the spiritual life by such means as lay in their power, and achieved a very high standard of character. What can we say to these things but this — that Christ appeared to them in another form? For where the Spirit of Jesus is, there is the revelation of Jesus — and the light that lighteth every man who cometh into this world is capable of streaming even through a pagan creed, of shining in the face of Buddha, of manifesting itself to sincere and honest souls everywhere: and without such a truth to sustain us it would be impossible to look upon the world at all, save with utter horror and despair.

And think of the many forms of religion in our own midst. So far as ecclesiastical forms go they are irreconcilable. Nay, more than that, we should lose by their complete fusion, for organic unity is not desirable, even were it possible. It is not desirable simply because men have, and must needs have, inherent differences from one another. Because we do see truth from different angles of vision, we must needs have a great variety of Christian organisations to express these different visions of truth. When Christ prayed that His flock might be one, it was not organic but spiritual unity that He desired. And that spiritual unity is attained when men do see the authentic vision of Christ — the Church is one simply by virtue of loyalty and love to Christ — and it matters nothing at all, except by way of consolation and encouragement, that each Christian organisation sees the Saviour in a different form.

But this let us all know, that we must see Christ or die in our sins. Until we see Him we are lost — lost as those men were lost, who had nothing left to live for, no hope in earth or heaven, no care for anything but to hasten back to the old sensual earthly life, which they had left at the call of Christ. To be carnally minded is death: to be spiritually minded is life and peace — and they were turning their backs on life, they were going back to the ways of death. And to them the Risen Life spoke: the Christ once more became manifest. What matter how He came, and in what form — the thing was, He did come, and they saw and believed. And for us let there be no further talk of forms — let us rather fix our whole mind on this one truth, we must believe or die. How

Christ shall show Himself to you I care not: in what form of Christian organisation you are likeliest to find the authentic vision of Christ, I will not even discuss — go where you will, worship as you like, join any church that seems most to meet your needs — but be content with nothing less than this, the actual revelation of Christ as Saviour, Atonement, Redeemer, to your own soul — for we must see Christ or perish, we must believe or die.

UTTER KNOWLEDGE IS UTTER LOVE

XI

UTTER KNOWLEDGE IS UTTER LOVE

"For He knew what was in man."—John ii. 25.

"Jesus knew from the beginning who they were that believed not, and who should betray Him."—John vi. 64.

THUS the Evangelist speaks of his Master, and it is a statement often repeated. Alone, of all those who have taught and led humanity, Christ had a comprehensive and adequate knowledge of men. He made no mistakes; before His luminous searching gaze the secrets of all hearts were revealed. He was betrayed, knowing that He was betrayed; crucified, foreseeing His crucifixion. Nothing in the final tragedy surprised Him; He had long before rehearsed every predetermined detail of His agony. And nothing in the last days of Christ is so singular and striking as this calm profound discernment. But it is really of a piece with all His life, for in all His dealings with the world, in the midst of a thousand plots and conspiracies, traps, ambushes, hypocrisies, flatteries disguising hatred, and adulation covering scorn, He was never deceived as to the motives and springs of human conduct—"He knew what was in man."

Now the point which interests us most in such a statement is this: how did Christ act under this terrible burden of knowledge? For our first instinctive thought is that such knowledge can only be regarded as a crushing burden. Who would care to know the intimate secrets of the lives that most closely touch his own, and would be willing that his own heart should be exposed in all its nakedness even to the most sympathetic eye? We all of us walk through the world more or less tricked out in disguises, and we are content that it should be so. It is not cynicism, but a profound distrust and almost fear of human nature which makes us anxious not to pry too deeply into the lives of others, for who knows what we might find there? Would our friend be still our friend if his whole heart were laid bare to us? Would love survive the absolute revelation of all that has made up the texture of a life? All the meannesses, sins, follies, lusts, vanities, errors, which from time to time have stained the heart? Has it not often happened that some man or woman has been driven by a sudden impulse into the confession of some secret vice or weakness to a friend, only to discover too late that the confession rang the death-knell of friendship? And it was not that the friend behaved badly either; he meant to behave well, he tried to do so; but inevitably there was an altered estimate, and life was never the same again. These are the facts of experience that make us think that adequate, complete, absolute knowledge of another would be a terrible thing, that for our own peace half-knowledge is better, that only in very rare instances where the soul is perfectly lucid and the temper divinely generous and unselfish, can it be good for us to know all that may be known about another. Observe then; Christ did know all about men; knew them to their last fibre; knew them to the last coil of being; knew them to the innermost secrecies of experience; yet He reverenced human nature, and all His relations with men and women were characterised of three great notes: Charity, Sympathy, and Hope.

Adequate knowledge of men taught Christ Charity toward them; think of that a moment. Take, for example, the relations of Christ with His disciples. He knew what was in such men as Peter and Judas. Peter did not know himself, but his Lord knew him thoroughly. Very early in their intimacy Christ had gauged aright the vanity, pride, and moral weakness of Peter; yet never did Jesus love Peter more than in that moment when He looked upon him with that look which broke the recreant disciple's heart. He knew what was in Judas; yet not once in the three years' ministry is there a harsh word against Judas; and when the final word is spoken which dismisses Judas from the discipleship it is not harsh, but ineffably tender, solemn, dignified, the reluctant verdict of outraged love that still loves. And so with all the disciples; there was enough of error and stupidity, of dull intractable lowness of thought and ideal, to hurt and offend Jesus grievously, yet He loved these men with a love stronger than death. How do we explain this constancy of love? The explanation is simple. Christ saw their virtues as well as their vices, their qualities as well as their defects; He saw not an aspect of a man, but the whole man as he was, and the large and candid vision produced the large and noble charity of His regard.

Here then is adequate knowledge inspiring not contempt but charity, and is not the lesson obvious? The longer I live the more clearly do I see that the harsh, contemptuous, uncharitable verdicts which we so often pass upon our fellow-creatures are almost always caused by inadequate knowledge. There is probably not a single person of our acquaintance who is not a good deal better than we suppose him, as we should readily discover if we knew him better. But alas, for us and him; we cannot restrain our tongues when we speak of him; we love to mock his peculiarities and his defects; we tell this and that caustic story at his expense; we know some spiteful little anecdote about his habits or his temper; so we ridicule, or avoid, or defame, or misapprehend, or neglect a man who may have many concealed qualities of character far finer and rarer than any we ourselves can boast. Some people seem to have a positive genius for discovering the worst side of worthy men; they scent a fault a mile off, and do not perceive a virtue when it is beneath their nose. There are faults enough, no doubt, in human nature, but is it a worthy thing or a kind thing to make it your chief business to discover and catalogue them? Nay, is it a just thing? Have we not all known moments of compunction when we have found that we have wholly misjudged some fellow-creature through a purposed ignorance? Suddenly we have come upon the tragic facts of his domestic life, some secret calamity nobly concealed through years, some burden heroically borne, some grief endured in self-respecting reticence, and then we have been ashamed of our careless jesting. The man we thought mean has had others depending on him of whom we have never heard; the man we thought rough in temper, has gone through seas of sorrow which would have overwhelmed a man less masterful. O, believe me, of all the forces most fatal to human brotherhood, there is none that works such evil as the gibing tongue, the spiteful narrow temper that fixes itself like a leech on the faults of others, the mean cynical habit of judging everyone, not by the best in them, but by the worst; and clearly of all tempers none can be more utterly un-Christlike. For Christ who knew all that was in man, never failed in charity to man; He who saw man most completely, loved man most perfectly. And so I repeat that the way to a larger charity towards others is better knowledge of them. You would not like others to judge you by your faults alone; judge not lest ye be judged. You would claim that if you have certain faults, at least you also possess some virtues; what you believe of yourself learn to believe of others too. I have had to do in public life with many men whom I have loved, with some who did not attract me, with a few whom I have disliked; but I profess that I never yet met the man who had not some quality in him which deserved esteem, and often enough I have learned to love the man whom I began by disliking, because I have come to know him better with the lapse of time. The one sovereign remedy for an uncharitable temper is wider knowledge of humanity; for He who loved and honoured mankind most was He who knew the most about men, the Saviour who knowing the worst, was never blind to the best, and ever judged men by their best rather than their worst.

Jesus knew not only imperfect people but evil people; He knew what was in them, and what He knew taught Him Sympathy for them. Think for a moment of Christ's treatment of that detested and forlorn class of the Jewish community known as harlots and publicans. There was no question about the facts of their lives, they were notorious and infamous. The life of the one was then what it is now, a gilded shame, a smiling misery, a tragic fact, but all the same a fact not named, tacitly connived at, even excused, but never pitied. The life of the publican was equally notorious; he was hated as the agent of a tyranny, and he was treated universally as an outcast. If a Pharisee had been asked to express his opinion of these people, we can imagine what he would have said. He would have considered them not worth a thought; they were wholly bad, the mere offal of humanity. Civilisation has its sewers, and sewers have their rats; they were the sewer-creatures of humanity, possibly answering some purpose in the universal scheme, but no more worth consideration than the sewer-rat. That was the Pharisee's view, that is still the way in which people of respectable virtues think of these miserables of humanity. Everyone knows that such creatures exist, but it is convenient to forget their existence. As for treating them as human, as having qualities not wholly despicable, as being amenable to any generous or pious impulses, that is absurd! Here is the bright street where the children of virtue walk clothed in shining raiment; below is the sewer and the rats, and it is nothing less than an insult to name the two in the same breath.

How did Jesus think about the matter? Why, with a daring originality which we have wholly failed to comprehend, even though we have read His words a thousand times. Notice one thing only which He says; He says that these were the very people who received Him most gladly, and showed themselves most sympathetic to His spirit and His message. If you will make careful note of the sort of sins which Christ most vehemently denounced, you will discover that He had much less to say about the sin of the publican and the outcast, than the sin of the Pharisee. And what was the chief sin of the Pharisee? It was contempt of humanity, a contempt which led him into every detestable variety of rancour, spite, and malice. To hate your brother or sister, to see no good in them, to treat them as incapable of good, to spurn them, to loathe them, to trample them under the feet of your own swollen spiritual pride, that was the sin of all sins to Jesus. He knew what was in man, and because He knew, He discerned in these despised people, qualities which were not despicable; veins of pure gold running through the clay; fountains of pity under the crust of debasement; generous and noble tempers, struggling through the opposition of much that was ignoble in life and habit, and He sympathised with them because He could comprehend them.

Jesus knew Human Nature as a whole, and the result of His knowledge was Faith in man.

"Faith in man"; it is a phrase very easy to utter, but it represents a temper very difficult to achieve and maintain. Think of the ignorance, stupidity, and ingratitude of man; his indifference to the labours of the wise and the sacrifices of the heroic; his inability or reluctance to follow truth with ardour or persistence; his carnal propensities, his perpetual sacrifice of the spiritual to the material, and his consequent contempt and even hatred of those who disturb his base apathy with the vision of spiritual progress or attainment; think not only of the follies of the ignorant, and the crimes of the stupid, but of the weaknesses and follies of the good themselves; and who does not feel a certain hopelessness fall upon him like a cloud, when he endeavours to look into the long vista of the future of humanity? How rarely is it that the historian, who has traced the vacillations of the human will, through the blunders and disasters of centuries, comes to his last page with unabated hope? How rarely is it that statesmen are hopeful men; how much oftener do they fall into acrid cynicism, and flout and jeer the nation they would lead, rather than hearten and encourage it? How often do even leaders in religious and moral progress lose heart, tacitly admitting that the evil of the world is too great for them, and that the folly of man is incurable. Everyone knows the French proverb, so often quoted by John Morley, that he who would work for his fellow-men should see as little as possible of them, and that proverb is the very essence of disappointed altruism. What it expresses really is, that while it is a duty to work for others, yet man is a poor creature, and hardly worth the trouble you take over him. You may do some little good by your toil, but never what you hoped, designed, or expected, for human stupidity will prove invincible in the long run. Faith in man

— no, it is a rare temper even in religious leaders; possible to the young perhaps, but increasingly difficult to the old, and in any case a temper not easy to maintain through a lifetime even by the most ardent of men.

Turn once more to the story of Jesus, and you find that He did maintain this temper of faith in man. He was despised and rejected of men, yet He had faith in man. He knew more than any other has ever known of the baseness of the human heart, yet He had faith in the perfectibility of man. His story is a story of infinite injustice, betrayal, and treachery; the noblest of the sons of men, yet is He treated as the basest; the wisest, He becomes the scorn of the foolish; the most magnanimous, yet is He the sport of the meanest; surely if anything could shake one's faith in humanity it would be such a tragedy as this! But Jesus died full of hope for men; and it is exquisitely characteristic of Him that His last act was to gladden the soul of the dying robber who hung beside Him on the Cross. How did Jesus maintain this temper? It was the result of His perfect knowledge of humanity. He knew what was in man, and He knew that there was enough of good and of the desire of good even in the basest to encourage hopefulness. And if you and I have grown contemptuous of men, is it not because we have ceased to know them, ceased to put ourselves in close contact with them? Ah, what so easy as to live one's life apart, to pay no attention to the wonderful spectacle of human nature as a whole, and so slowly to absorb that miasma of cynicism, which is the inevitable punishment of a selfish mode of thought, and an isolated mode of life? You will always find that those who have most faith in man are those who come into closest contact with man at his worst. I have never yet met a City Missionary or a Salvation Army Captain, or even a prison-visitor, whose eyes did not light up with faith in man, as he related some story of pity among the degraded, or kindness between the destitute. If you have lost faith in human nature, and want to recover it, the best suggestion that I can make is: Go down to some mission among the poor or the depraved, armed with kindness, and there amidst the dust and ashes of a half-ruined humanity, you will discover so much of goodness and greatness still left, that you will have no doubt about the inherent greatness of human nature. You know something of the outside of these men — their rags, their dirt, their physical debasement; learn to know what is *in* them, and you will find in the lowest, something to reverence and respect. And at least be sure of this; faith in God is quite impossible without faith in man. It was not for nothing that Christ put duty to our neighbour, the cup of cold water given to a child, the food to the hungry, the clothes to the naked, in the forefront of all piety; we cannot be in a right relation to God unless we are in right relation to our brother man, for if we love not our brother whom we have seen, how can we love God whom we have not seen?

"Thou knowest all things, thou knowest that I love thee," said Simon Peter, and so the last suggestion may be the *Consolations* of this theme. Do you recall what were the bitterest moments of childhood? They were moments when the heart rankled with the sense of injustice, and what caused that sense of injustice? The conviction that we were not comprehended, that there was a side of our conduct that we could not explain, that our real motives were very different from our apparent motives. Peter knew all that this meant, but the perfect knowledge that Christ had of him was his consolation. "To know all is to forgive all," is one of those ancient proverbs which man has had to learn through his own agony. It is imperfect knowledge we fear most, for that means imperfect understanding. But where knowledge is perfect we have much less to fear, for He who knows the worst of us, knows equally the best. "Thou knowest all things, thou knowest that I love thee."

Most men, in reviewing their lives, have a feeling that if everything were fully known, if the nature of their temptations were understood, and the whole struggle of their existence, if they were judged with a comprehending sympathy, which gave credit for the best in them, as well as blame for the worst, things might not go so ill with them after all. The errors in a human court of justice are always the errors of imperfect knowledge. Some poor creature is pilloried for judgment, and it is all a question of evidence, rarely of motive, never of temptation. Nor in the human court of justice is there any room for moral discernment. Morally, the blow struck in anger, which causes death, is much less reprehensible than the cool and calculated roguery which wrecks a hundred homes, and escapes with a few months' imprisonment. But human judgment takes no count of what is in the man; if it did there is many a man arraigned for murder who would be lightly punished, and many a man arraigned for a lifetime of cruel devastating fraud who would be hanged. Such is human justice, but God's justice is wholly different. He who tries us at the last assize will know what is in us, will know us intimately, absolutely, and so we do not fear. So at least David argued in that wonderful 139th Psalm; the God who knows his downsitting and his uprising, and all his thoughts, will show him more mercy than one who only judged him from the outside, and partially. Once more we see that perfect knowledge makes not for despair but faith. "If I am to be judged rightly, let me be judged by one who knows all about me," is what we all say; he who knows all will treat us more justly, more kindly than he who knows only a little, and that not the best about us. To such a judgment we can resign ourselves with confidence; we can meet our Lord without fear, knowing that if we are punished, it will be punishment in which we ourselves shall acquiesce, being confidently assured that the Judge of all the earth will do right.

To say this perhaps sounds arrogance, but it is not; it is rather the sweet calm faith of the little child who is not afraid to meet his father. "My father will understand me," says the child; "he knows me in all my motives, he comprehends my temperament, he will make no errors." "*Utter knowledge is but utter love,*" says Tennyson, and it is a profound truth. If Christ who knew the worst of men found in the worst something that was worthy, something that was loveable, may we not humbly trust that in the great day of judgment He who knows us utterly will also love us utterly? May we not turn aside from the evil dreams of harsh theology, from the misjudgments and misapprehensions of men, to the faithful Creator and Father of our spirits, saying with confidence, "Into Thy hands, I commit my spirit"? And when we are called to stand, as we so often are, by the death-bed of those who have manifested no very vigorous spiritual instincts, who go out into the unknown with no definite profession of faith, but taking with them a record of human faithfulness, and love, and generosity, marred, no doubt, by many errors, may we not then find consolation in the thought that He who knows what is in man will deal with these imperfect children far more wisely and tenderly than we can do? "Utter knowledge is but utter love," and

"The love of God is broader
Than the measures of man's mind,
And the heart of the Eternal
Is most wonderfully kind."

Because God knows what is in man He loves man with an everlasting love. Because God is Light, God is Love, and there we rest, persuaded that what we have committed to Him, He will keep against the eternal day, and that neither death nor life can part us from the love of God which is in Christ Jesus our Lord.

THE PERSONAL FACTOR IN RELIGION

XII

THE PERSONAL FACTOR IN RELIGION

"For My sake and the Gospel's."—Mark viii. 35.

WHEN you speak of Christianity you are not speaking of a philosophic creed, or an organised system of thought, but of a form of passion, uniting Christ with individuals. Judaism is a composite creed, the work of many hands; Christianity is Christ. The apostolic life of Paul had its source in one thing, and one alone, personal loyalty to a Master. The same thing may be said of all the great saints and heroes of Christianity through the ages; of men as far apart in type as Xavier and Wesley, as Francis of Assisi and Chalmers of New Guinea — they speak a common language when they speak of Christ. They are not disciples in the sense in which a student is the disciple of a master; their whole life is lived in and through Christ, they are knit closer to Him than to any earthly friend or lover; their lives are lived, their sufferings are endured, their victories achieved, for Christ's sake.

For Christ's sake: the phrase is so familiar to us that its freshness is exhausted. We have said it so often in hymns and worship that it has ceased to convey any definite meaning to our minds. Nevertheless it is one of the most striking phrases in the vocabulary of human thought. It records a revolution in men's ideas of religion. It simplifies Christianity, so that the humblest, and least subtle of mind, can understand it. It is the secret of Christ's hold upon the human race.

Think of these two things to begin with:—

First, that this phrase "For My sake" constitutes a motive for action which is quite peculiar to Christianity. No other great religious teacher has ever told the world to do right for his sake; but for right's sake and truth's sake. Neither Buddha nor Mohammed ever made the reception of the truths they taught contingent upon personal loyalty to themselves; they regarded their doctrine as potent enough to demand belief apart from all personal emotions. Neither did Paul, even when pleading with his converts with an almost womanly tenderness of feeling, ever beg them to pursue any given line of conduct for his sake; the most he dared to say was that he in Christ's stead besought them to be reconciled to God. Alone, among all known religions, Christianity centres in a person, makes its chief motive love to a person, and counts even the proper apprehension of truth as of less importance than warm and loyal passion to that person. The keynote of Christianity is thus loyalty to Christ, and its two great watchwords are, "*Lovest thou Me?*" "*Follow Me.*"

A second outstanding characteristic of Christianity is, that pure and lofty as it is in point of ethics, yet those ethics would be relatively unimpressive without the character and story of Christ Himself. His precepts are exquisite, but they gain all their real force from His own life. Others have told us to love our enemies, but it is only when we stand at the Cross and hear Him blessing a thief, and praying for His murderers that we comprehend what He meant. Others have taught us pity for the sinful, but the true scope of such a precept is only felt when we see Him eating and drinking with sinners, deliberately seeking their company, and saying to a guilt-laden woman, "Neither do I condemn thee, go in peace." And as it is with His precepts so it is with His doctrines. The benignant fatherhood of God becomes intelligible when we mark the perfect benignity of Christ's own character; and His great doctrine of immortality and life eternal passes from speculation into fact when we stand beside His own empty sepulchre. Thus we may say that had Christ only given us what the man of genius gives us, the fine fruit of His mind, His teachings would have had little or no power to move the world, and none whatever to create a revolution in human thought. It is the spectacle of His own life and example that has fascinated the mind of men; and He Himself was well aware that the true and moving revelation He brought the world, was not so much what He taught, as what He was. In the phrase "For my sake" He makes love to Himself the one supreme and abiding motive of all Christian life, duty, and service.

Now let me try to amplify and explain what these statements mean. Men are continually seeking, with insatiable curiosity, to understand what Christianity is, and what it really means to be a Christian. Books are written on it, sermons preached, lectures delivered in universities and seats of culture, and so extraordinary is the interest excited by this theme, that full as the world is with books about Christianity, every year adds a new library to Christian literature; and often as the theme has been discussed, no Sabbath dawns, when millions of men and women are not gathered together for a fresh discussion of the theme. Is it possible to compress all this mass of thought into some brief, clear, axiomatic form? Can I give to any man who asks the plain question "What is it to be a Christian?" a plain answer, an answer clear, convincing, and decisive? I think I can. To be a Christian is to be brought into such personal relation with Christ that henceforth the soul is obedient to His authority, and all truth is seen through Christ, and the whole life is lived, in all its acts and tempers, for Christ's sake. It is not a question of creed, dogmas, proofs, and evidences, but of personal relationship to Christ, and personal loyalty to Him. The personal factor is the controlling factor in the whole problem. Christianity is nothing more or less than the story of the human soul in its personal relationship to Christ; that is the centre, from which that wide line of circumference is drawn which includes literatures, philosophies, histories, and the long struggle of causes and nations.

Think, for example, of the Personal Factor in Christ's own Earthly Ministry.

The narrative of the earliest acts of that ministry is contained in the first chapter of St. John's Gospel, and it concerns itself with a group of five men in their personal relationship to Christ.

Christ appears full of grace and truth before the startled and delighted eyes of John the Baptist, of Andrew, of Peter, of Philip and Nathaniel, and except in the case of Nathaniel not a word is spoken in exposition of Christ's claims or authority. Neither is there a single word spoken to either of the five men on any one of those distinctive doctrines which were to compose Christ's gospel. That gospel lies, as yet, folded in the silence of Christ's heart. No one of these men can by any possibility suspect what the outlines of that Gospel are to be. Yet what happens? Christ no sooner appears than their hearts cleave to Him. John hails Him as the Lamb of God; Andrew and Peter leave their fishing nets instantly when He says "Follow Me"; Philip makes haste to claim for Christ a Messiahship of which He Himself has said nothing, and Nathaniel exclaims, "Thou art the Son of God, Thou art the King of Israel." Not a word spoken by Christ, not a dogma nor a doctrine defined, not a word as to what kind of service it is to which He pledges these men, yet they follow Him instinctively, and why? Because they feel that Christ is the Gospel. Nothing He can say to them can affect them so much as what He is. They love Him as only noble souls can love; with a passion that forgets and extinguishes self; with a swift and beautiful loyalty; and thus the love of Christ constrains them henceforth to live only in the presence of Christ and for His sake.

Try and recall for a moment the scenes of Christ's active ministry, and you will find that there is one characteristic which runs through all — His ministry is constantly addressed to individuals. There are sermons on the Mount and beside the Lake; great public utterances such as you might expect from a religious reformer; but always something else, personal contact with individuals. Great multitudes followed Him in admiration, but His converts, the men and women who are to spread His doctrine and form the nucleus of His Church, are the results of His personal touch on individual lives. Mary Magdalene is won not by sermons on the Mount, but by the gracious tender touch of Christ, which delivered her disordered mind from the cloud of madness, her haunted soul from the spectres of despair. The woman who is a sinner is drawn to Christ, not by the publication of His doctrines, which would have moved her not at all; but by the reverence and awe and penitent love He awoke in her by His mere presence, and this moved her to the depths. It is the same all through the ministry of Christ, from first to last; with Nicodemus, with His disciples, with the dying thief; it is always Christ Himself, not the things He says, that overwhelms the soul; it is the power of His own personality acting on the souls of men, that draws them to Himself and changes the current of their lives.

Notice also that in His ministry among men, Christ constantly uses the language of the affections. In the whole life of Christ, and in His whole ministry, what do you find the most distinctive thing, the unique thing, its feature, its characteristic? I find that it is the place He gives to love. It is of the love of God He speaks when He names God; it is loving-kindness in humble men He praises — the hungry fed, the sick comforted, the prisoner visited, the cup of cold water given to a child; these are the superlative acts of life by which character is revealed, by which eternal destinies are determined. It is the power of love in the heart of woman which He distinguishes as woman's divinest gift. He defends Mary from the attack of Judas, because her extravagance is the beautiful extravagance of love; He forgives a woman, whose sins are many, because she loves much. And it is the language of the affections which He uses when He pleads with His followers, "Will ye also go away?"— when He says to Peter "Lovest thou me?"— and when He makes Himself the universal object of all love by saying, "Inasmuch as men do kindnesses to those who are poor as He was poor, and hungry and thirsty, and in need, as He was in need, they do it unto Him."

> "For love He wrought,
> Who sowed with springing bloom our mortal graves.
> Only with hatred and its ills He fought,
> Claiming for seraphs those who toiled as slaves.
> For love He wrought. Be faith or clear or dim,
> He waits in love for all who follow Him."

For my sake. Is it not the most intimate language of the affections that Christ uses here? "*For my sake*": the very phrase is sanctified by all the mystery and sweetness of human love. "*For my sake*": it is the appeal of the dying mother to her child, of parted lovers between whom oceans are about to roll, of martyred patriots, surrendering their memory and their cause to their disciples. No man has begun to live in any true or noble sense until he has begun to live for the sake of others. That is the supreme and simple truth of Christianity. Men must be lifted out of self-love, and they can only achieve that deliverance through love for another. Therefore Christ speaks as a lover, and all that He can do for the souls of men is done when men love Him, and begin to live for His sake. This is the unique achievement of Christ. He is loved as no other was ever loved. This is what excited the wonder of Napoleon when he said, "Cæsar, Charlemagne and I have founded empires on force; they have perished; Jesus Christ founded an empire on love, and at this hour millions would die for Him." Here is the personal factor in Christianity, which so colours and controls everything, that all else is unimportant. Christ makes His appeal, "Live for my sake," and men through all the ages answer, "For me to live is Christ, to die is gain."

Pass from the ministry of Christ, to that ministry which by common consent is next to Christ's the most wonderful in human history, the ministry of Paul. What do you find here that is extraordinary? Once more the personal factor, the personal relation between Paul and Jesus, colouring every thought of the apostle and governing all his life.

Paul had a very wide theology, and some of you may say, a very difficult and abtruse theology, ranging through many subtleties of the intellect, and penetrating the profoundest secrets of time and eternity. True, but you will find that wide as Paul's theology was, he had a very narrow and simple creed. He believed not more than two or three things, but he believed them intensely. The mission of his life was to go on repeating these two or three things till they were impressed upon the consciousness of mankind. Before the Jewish Sanhedrin and Roman governors, in the conclave of the Apostles, and in the presence of the sceptical philosophers of Athens; in his familiar correspondence with his friends; in his controversial treatises, in his conversation with acquaintances made in travel, with soldiers who had charge of him, and officers of the empire sent to investigate his case, he continually affirms the two or three things that made the creed on which his life was built. What were these things? That he had seen Christ in the spirit, and had heard the voice of Christ, which he had never heard in the flesh. That he knew Christ was risen from the dead, for he had felt the power of His resurrection. That his own life was changed in every fibre, and that he was converted, by the contact of Christ with his own soul. There is Paul's creed, the reality of contact with Christ. How little the teachings of Christ, considered only as teachings, counted with Paul, you may judge by the strange fact that he does not quote a single parable of Christ's, or refer to a single incident of the Galilean ministry, nor contribute anything whatever to our knowledge of His earthly life. Why was this? Because Paul's relation to Christ was not in the least like the ordinary relations of the scholar to the intellectual master, the scholar who expounds his master's philosophy, or re-defines his teaching. No, it is not the tradition of Christ's earthly life that shapes the life of Paul, it is daily, hourly contact with Christ. He has been lifted out of himself by a wave of love that has brought him to the bosom of Christ. He has found the love and life of Christ flowing into his own life and transfiguring it. He not only believes *what* Christ has said in beatitude and parable, he knows *Whom* he has believed. And that is conversion — contact with Christ. It is not belief in something Christ has taught or done; it is surrender to Christ. It is the giving of the heart to Christ — that old evangelistic phrase which no change of thought can render obsolete — an act performed in the realm of the affections, a surrender to love, so that henceforth you live, not for self but for Christ, and for His sake.

That old evangelistic theology had many phrases which were truer than we think, and as I grow older I begin to realise how true they are. It spoke of coming to Jesus. It spoke of appropriating faith. It taught men to sing —

> " I the chief of sinners am,
> But Jesus died for me,"

thus connecting my sin, done but yesterday, with the death of Jesus, suffered centuries ago upon the Tree. There is not one of these phrases that is not true, when you remember that the source of Christianity is personal contact with Christ. You do appropriate all the grace of Christ to yourself when you let your heart go out to Him in love. You do make His death a death for you, when you feel that He is not only the world's Saviour, but your Saviour. The Christ whom Paul knew, not by discussions about His person, or memories of His teachings, but by personal contact, spirit with spirit, soul to soul, in the rapture of love and self-surrender, may be known to you by the same means. Try the method, and see if it be not true. Let your heart choose Christ at this moment, and see if the answering love of Christ does not thrill you through and through. Centuries do not alter the fact of this experience; still Christ says "Love me, live for my sake," and still men rise from their knees to sing in a flood of happy tears —

> "'Tis done, the great transaction's done.
> I am my Lord's, and He is mine,
> He called me and I followed on,
> Charmed to confess the Voice Divine."

And then lastly I want you to realise the truth to which I have already referred, that in knowing Christ by personal contact, you for the first time know what His doctrine really means. Living for Christ's sake, you begin to see all life in and through Christ. This truth is admirably put by a man who cannot be counted a friend of Christianity, Mr. Grant Allen, in his "*Evolution of the Idea of God,*" when he says that it was not the doctrine of a Resurrection that converted Western Europe, but the fact that the Apostles of Christ said, "We tell you a tale of a real life, and recent: we present you with a specimen of actual resurrection." What can convince me of the Resurrection of Christ? Nothing but vital contact with Christ, when I am trying to live in the daily love of Christ, and for His sake. And thus living for Christ's sake all life is seen through Christ. I measure my daily duty by His spirit of duty, I interpret my disciplines by His Cross, I see my grave in the light of His illumined sepulchre. Living for Christ's sake, I more and more perceive that His life outlines mine, that which He knew of the Divine presence I may know, His way of thinking is my way, and His final victory over death will be my victory too.

Everyone knows something of the beautiful and wonderful work of the Solar spectrum. Upon the spectrum are reproduced various lines, which until 1860 were a puzzle to the astronomer. Then a discovery was made which cast a new light upon the universe, for it was found that these lines stood for certain elements in the sun, which exists also on the earth. Think of it, upon this tiny film, the sun, millions of miles as it is away, writes the record of its nature, and behold that nature is composed of the same elements as this little earth. Even so Christ mirrors Himself upon the believing heart. He is far away, in the realms of risen life, yet His life corresponds with ours. What were truths and duties, disciplines and victories for Him, are the same for us, and all our life lies explained in His, all our life is illumined by the light of His most perfect life. The moment contact is established with Christ we see our life through Christ's life, and our life shines glorious in the light of His.

The personal factor in religion; practically for you and me no other factor counts. A thousand poets have written on love, but you will learn more of love in the kiss of a little child, in the pressure of a kind hand, in the soft glance of loyal and tender eyes, than you will in reading all the exquisite and all the true things written about love since the world began. It is so with Christ. Christianity is meaningless to you till you feel the contact of the soul with Christ:

> The love of Jesus, what it is,
> None but His loved ones know.

In one of the greatest spiritual confessions of our generation, "*The Story of an African Farm*," Olive Schreiner pours out her heart in this exceeding bitter cry.

"Why am I alone, so hard, so cold? It is eating my soul to the core, self, self, self! I cannot bear this life! I cannot breathe! I cannot live! Will nothing free me from myself? I want something great and pure to lift me to itself."

Christ is the answer to that cry. Love for Him is the great and pure passion that lifts us out of self. All that bitter loneliness which tortured the soul of the brilliant writer, would have passed away forever, had she known how to kneel at the Cross of Christ. To give the heart to Christ, to surrender the whole soul to Him, to come to Jesus, to live for Christ's sake — once more I say the old Evangelistic phrases ring true, they rest upon the experience of millions, and may be true to you also, if you will act upon them. " Come unto Me, and I will give you rest,"— rest in deliverance from self, rest in surrender to God — so Christ speaks still, so He speaks to you, all ye who are weary and heavy-laden, and may God give you grace to find the peace and joy of the life surrendered to your Saviour, and henceforth lived in His service, and for His sake.

THE POWER OF PRINCIPLE

XIII

THE POWER OF PRINCIPLE

"How then can I do this great wickedness, and sin against God."— Gen. xxxix. 9.

THOSE who write and speak especially to youth have often drawn up interesting categories of its qualities and characteristics — its energy, sincerity, buoyancy, unbounded aspiration, and so forth; they have not so often observed that youth is peculiarly the period of temptation. The man who has attained to middle age, if he be not altogether a fool, has usually attained to some degree of sober wisdom, but sobriety is not among the gifts of youth. Rather youth is the period of inebriation, of excess, of extravagance, when nothing is seen in its real outlines, or apprehended in its true nature. The first full draught of life which a man drinks is not only exhilarating — it is intoxicating. It is bliss to be alive; all the world shines transfigured through a golden mist, and is as a mirage in which the very pits of Sodom are magically made to take the outline of the Delectable Mountains themselves. It is small wonder that in this general ferment and tumult of the nature, youth should find itself allured by a thousand temptations. To taste, to see, to handle, to know what life is; to experience the things of which men have written and talked; to drink the cup of pleasure to the dregs; to enjoy, before the evil days come when the tired and satiated heart says, "I have no pleasure in them"; to plunge deep into the stinging tide of all human experience — all this appeals irresistibly to the frank paganism of youth. And thus it is that youth, in its first delirium of living often rushes straight towards ruin, and before it has had time to count the cost, knows itself bankrupt of those qualities which give life its true serenity and triumph.

Now that which is true of all youth, was no doubt true of Joseph. In that far-gone period when he lived, moral restraint was much weaker than it is to-day, and the mere pagan joy of life proportionately stronger. Consider what it meant for such a youth to be suddenly introduced to the corrupting and luxurious life of Egypt. From the simple patriarchal life of the plains he was violently separated by a series of bitter vicissitudes. He was a peasant of genius, suddenly made a citizen of a complex civilisation; and such an instance as that of Robert Burns may serve to remind us of the grave perils of the position. If he had ever sighed for a larger life than that of the agriculturist and cattle breeder, now he had it. If he had ever felt his veins athirst for the pleasures of life, now that thirst might be easily gratified. He was among a people who loved pleasure, and who knew little of sin. The standards by which they measured life were wholly different from those to which he had been accustomed. Probably there was not one among his acquaintances who would not have laughed at his scruples, and have jeeringly told him to do in Egypt as Egypt did. If you would discover the place in which life is most corrupt, morals most easy, the desires of the flesh least restrained, you would go first to the precincts of a Court where luxury, idleness, and the sense of being freed from the ordinary social restrictions are nearly always found, and it was in such an atmosphere Joseph lived. The peasant of genius in the house of Potiphar — conceive the situation. How easy to snatch at forbidden pleasures, which not one of his acquaintances would have resisted or would have even thought it politic to resist. But Joseph did resist, and as the sequel showed his whole future life and the existence of his people, depended on his resistance. Of course he did not know that; no man is able to foresee that he is making history. But one thing he did know — he knew what right and wrong were, and he knew that he was accountable to God for all his actions. His first instinctive words are, "How can I do this great wickedness, and sin against God?" And when we come to weigh these words, and measure the whole situation, what we see is this: that the whole secret of Joseph's triumph was that he was a youth of principle. That was what saved him in the trying hour; that is what can alone save us in the moments of great temptation — he had principles and he was faithful to them.

First of all, *What then is Principle?* Is it something elemental, fundamental, which is taken for granted in all reasoning, and thus becomes a standard of thought or conduct. In every science you have principles, and until these are accepted science can teach you nothing. In every art you have principles, and until you have mastered these, accepted these, and throned them as unalterable, no knowledge of art is possible. Euclid gives you the principles of mathematics before he proposes the problem, for it is by the application of the principles that the problems are to be solved. You may have plenty of aspiration for art or science, but the first element of progress is not aspiration, but obedience. So in the affairs of the soul, there are fundamental and axiomatic things which we must admit before we can give any right shape to conduct; for religion is not primarily an aspiration, but a submission or an obedience. Joseph had a sure grasp on two principles; that he was accountable to God for his actions, and that certain actions were wicked; and in the most tremendous hour of moral crisis which he knew he was saved by these principles.

We sometimes say of a man, "He is an unprincipled man"; what is it we mean? We mean that he is unscrupulous. There is hardly a more damning epithet that can be applied to a human creature. Such a man proves himself in every relation of life utterly untrustworthy and unreliable. If he be a business man there is no knavery which he will not practise on occasion; if he sign an agreement to-day he will set to work to-morrow to repudiate it, or make it nugatory; if you trust him, he betrays you; if you confide your interests to him he will sacrifice them the moment self-interest interferes; and not because he deliberately means to be a knave or a thief but simply because there is no fundamental honesty about him, which gives a governing principle to conduct. If he be a workman, he works only when the master's eye is upon him; he puts honest work only where it can be seen, and goes home whistling from his knavish work, utterly careless of the fact that he has built a house or laid a drain in such a way that the lives of men and women must be sacrificed to his purposed incompetency. If he be a politician he learns to lie so glibly that he hardly knows when he lies; he uses any weapon that comes to his hand without a thought of its nature; he drifts into wars which a moment of firm thought might have prevented, and in the long run he does his country more lasting damage than could be wrought by the wildest anarchist, or the most revolutionary of honest demagogues. And when you come to the social aspects of life, the wrongs wrought by lack of principle are even more agonising though perhaps more circumscribed in their effects. George Eliot has sketched us such a man with inimitable skill in the Tito Melema of her great novel, "Romola." She takes pains to show us that Tito was not, in the ordinary sense of the term, a bad man. He has many engaging and quite fascinating qualities. He is brilliant, joyous, refined, fond of giving pleasure to others, and eager to make himself friendly and serviceable. But in his heart he has no principle, no love of virtue, no respect for duty. The moment his personal interests are menaced he turns to adamant. To save himself he will sacrifice anyone; at the root of all his gaiety and fascinating manners, there is an utterly unscrupulous self-interest. He is no libertine, but he will ruthlessly wreck the life of the little blue-eyed contadina who pleases him with her child-like ways. He is not a brute; yet he will cast off his benefactor — with real regret — the moment his presence becomes inconvenient. He does not wish to betray or injure anyone; he would much rather not do it; but he has no real principle of honour or of virtue to deter him from the course that seems pleasant or expedient. And so the man goes through life wrecking the peace of all who know him, and finally is wrecked himself — and why? For want of principle. Had he but known how to say, "This is wickedness and sin against God"— had he learned to set his daily conduct in the light of God's purity, and said, "How can I sin against God?" all would have been different, and both for himself and others infinite sorrow and infinite tragedy might have been averted.

We see, then, what Principle means; it means a moral and spiritual standard which is sincerely accepted and rigidly obeyed. It gives us a power of moral discrimination, and enables us to say, "This may be a pleasure, but it is also wickedness." It gives us an awe-struck sense of responsibility to the unseen God, and enables us to say, "How can I sin against God?" And it becomes clear at once that such a principle working in a man's heart, such a moral standard obediently accepted, must necessarily alter and exalt the whole nature of a man's conduct. The business man knows then that the eye of God is on his ledger, and the workman makes his work good because he would feel himself dishonoured if he did not. The statesman in hours of difficulty consoles himself that certain things are inevitably and eternally right; that it is better to fail in the right than to succeed in the wrong; and that while expediency is man's wisdom, righteousness is God's. The ordinary man in all the social tests of life is lifted beyond the reach of temptations which offer momentary pleasures and advantages, because he sees life in a nobler perspective and has learned the inner joy of a virtue that is unstained, and an integrity which is uncorrupted. To such men right and wrong are no sounding phrases, they are the only abiding realities. Eternity and the thought of eternal things, becomes to them at once inspiration, restraint, and impulse. And so when they are suddenly brought face to face with some great temptation; when the Venus-vision of the flesh flashes on their startled eyes, when the sweet corrupt odours of forbidden pleasure assail their senses, when the snare is spread for the feet, and the bait held at their lips — they have a power by which they conquer, they have a spell before which the Venus-vision melts into thin air — they are able to fall back upon their sense of right, their sense of God, and to say, "How can I do this wickedness, and sin against God?" And they cannot do it; they simply CAN NOT; because a higher power holds them in its grasp, and a nobler vision gives them instant mastery over the base and the corrupting vision.

So much, perhaps, we accept and acknowledge; but now notice another thing, viz.: That it is only by moral principle that men conquer in such hours as these. It is as impossible to acquire sudden virtue as sudden heroism. Behind every human act there lies a history, and the act is the fruit of the history. Grapes do not grow upon thorns, nor figs on thistles, said Jesus — by which He meant that character rules conduct. Men do not always remember this. They suppose that if a great temptation came to them they would find some sort of magical power to resist it. But a man never finds in his heart the flower he has not planted there; he never finds the grape upon the thorn, or the fig upon the thistle. All principle means a slow accretion of will, thought and conviction; the gradual emergence from the fermenting chaos of a man's nature of the solid and impregnable elements on which he can build and rest; and in the great crises of temptation it is only by force of principle that we can be saved.

We see how true this is when we remember that all great temptations are sudden. On that memorable day when Joseph faced the great temptation of his life, he faced it without warning. There was not a hint in that fair Egyptian dawn that anything tragic was about to happen. No fellow-servant or officer of the household had breathed a word to put him on his guard. He rose as he had done on a hundred other mornings; rejoicing in his strength, full of the gladness of life, warmed and nerved by ambitious dreams, already seeing his life successful; he rose, and prayed to the God of Israel, and went about his duties in a quiet glow of health and energy. If he had known what was about to happen he might have braced himself for the hour, and have called up all the resources of his prudence and his will. But life gives very few of us the chance of inventing a deliberate strategy against a coming battle. We are taken unawares; we must fight as we stand. The days of destiny come, but they cast no shadow before. A man goes out in the morning to the city utterly ignorant that before night the great battle of his life will be fought. He goes out honest — he may come back a thief; he goes out virtuous — he may come back with a stain upon him that all his after life may not obliterate. The subtle antagonist with whom we have to deal gives us no time for preparation; he delights in surprises; the bolt falls out of the blue sky, the arrow flies through the clearest noon. Is it not plain then that to be prepared at all for temptation, we must be always prepared? And how are we to be prepared but by that daily, hourly attitude of mind which makes virtue dear to us and God real? And what does this mean but that it is principle alone that can save us in the sudden shock? If Joseph had had to begin to be religious on that fateful morning, nothing could have saved him; it was because he *was* religious, because he had lived his young life in stainless virtue, that he had resources to fall back on now, and stood fast in the evil day.

There is perhaps nothing in life more tragic than these sudden and overwhelming moral defeats which happen to men. It is no exaggeration to say that often enough a moment decides a destiny. A man rises without the least purpose of wrong-doing in his thoughts; he has lived in prudent virtue all his days; yet by nightfall he has done that which makes him loathe himself. We who look upon the amazing, the tragic spectacle, cannot understand it. We hear the growing whisper that couples his name with infamy, and we say, "It is impossible, it is incredible!" But usually there is no mystery in it at all; if we had known the man better we should not be incredulous. And when we do get at the real facts of the case all mystery disappears. We find then that there has been a long process of sapping and undermining before the crash came; that the man never really had a love of virtue or a detestation of vice; that he had been accustomed to read books which peopled his mind with corrupting images; that he had played with fire in his thoughts a thousand times; that his virtue was a part of his clothes, not a thing inherent in himself; that his religion was at best an æsthetic emotion: that, in fact, he had not a single, clearly defined principle which he could call his own. A building will stand a long time after it is undermined; so a man may stand a long time without any solid foundation of principle. But some day the undermined house falls all at once, and great is the fall of it — and this is, in brief, the usual history of those tragic downfalls, those sudden and total collapses of character and reputation, which to the outsider seem so incredible and amazing.

I say that men do not realise this fact, and it is because they do not, that they court defeat upon the battlefield of life. Thus, perhaps, some one says, "But surely prudence would be sufficient to save a man in such a crisis," and it is by no means uncommon to find men arguing that morality is really only a code of prudence after all. No doubt it is true that a man in his sane mind can readily perceive that certain sins are highly imprudent; no doubt also morality finds a certain sanction in prudence. But if virtue be nothing more than a glorified instinct of prudence, it will be of small avail when the inflamed blood of youth surges through the brain. Besides, the sin may appear so secret and so incapable of discovery that prudence may have nothing to say against it; and in any case the man who trusts to prudence only, will find himself arguing with the tempter, which is always the first step in submitting to the temptation. No! merely prudential considerations, however plain, are not strong enough to save us; and are especially inapplicable to youth, whose temper is usually at the furthest possible remove from prudence. Or, again, a man may say, "A spirit of true culture will preserve men from succumbing to such gross temptations as this of Joseph's." Will it? Alas, there is no delusion more absurd, and none so absolutely contradicted by the facts of life. No doubt culture is of great use in human discipline; it redeems the mind from emptiness, it surrounds it with a zone of intellectual interests, it creates a certain fastidiousness of taste which is offended by a temptation that is wholly gross and vulgar. But what if the temptation be neither gross nor vulgar? What if Venus wears the garments of the Angel of Light? And what of the men who in every age have joined culture of the mind with corruption of morals, fine manners with infamous vices, the thoughts of the Philosopher with the acts and habits of the Satyr?

Only a week or two ago, I heard of the case of a man, well-born, well-bred, highly educated, and on the brink of marriage, who in a single week drank himself to death in circumstances of unspeakable infamy. This man was a scholar, with a cultivated taste for the best forms of literature; he read his Greek Testament day by day, and when his books were examined after his death they consisted mainly of books on religion, curiously mixed with the filthiest of French novels. Exactly what happened to send him to his tragic end with such rapidity no one will ever know; but it was clear that a sudden temptation had overwhelmed him, and that neither the fastidious taste of the gentleman nor the culture of the scholar had had the least power to restrain him from plunging into the abyss. And when I think of the Greek Testament and the scrofulous French novel lying side by side in that man's library, I see another thing, that mere religiosity has as little power to save men from gross sin as culture. Do not suppose that because you go to church you are any the less likely to be overwhelmed in the evil hour. Do not imagine because you take a certain intellectual interest in religion, you are safe from the fiery darts of the wicked one. Joseph might have been the most cultured man in Egypt and the most interested student of her religion, but neither of these things would have saved him from a seduction so potent, so terrible, and so unexpectedly thrust upon him. No! once more I say, principle, and principle alone can save you in such hours as these. You must have something fundamental on which you can fall back — a belief, a conviction, a habit of thought; and this Joseph had. He knew the thing was wicked — that was enough; he knew that God would see what he did, and he dared not sin under the very eye of God. "How can I do this great wickedness, and sin against God?" he cried, and what neither prudence nor culture could have done for him, religious principle did.

There is yet one final train of thought suggested by this episode in the life of Joseph. There can be no doubt it was part of the discipline he endured in achieving that final greatness of character which made him one of the most memorable men in human history. The superficial man will probably say, "Why are such temptations permitted in a world where God is supposed to rule? If God wishes me to be pure, why doesn't He keep me pure?" Simply because you are a man, not a puppet, and because purity cannot truly be said to exist without the conquest of impurity, as light cannot be said to exist without darkness. We have all seen a boy sail a kite. The kite soars against the wind, and the tighter the string is held the harder the kite tugs at it, and the higher it soars. So it is with us; we can hardly be said to possess virtue till we find ourselves in active opposition with something that is not virtue. When the kite sails with a loose string it drops, because there is not enough opposition to keep it afloat; and when men have no odds against them in life, nothing to draw out their vital force of opposition, they also soon trail along the ground. This is the meaning of temptation; it is discipline. We do not enter the world ready-made; we are engaged in the making of ourselves, and in the process, temptation must needs play a tremendous part. To blame temptation, therefore, is merely childish and foolish, for what great life has ever yet been lived that did not grapple with the ghostly adversary, and win its greatness out of wrong resisted, evil overcome? And if we do not yet realise this, if we weakly blame circumstances instead of ourselves for our misdoings, let this great saying of St. Bernard's bring correction and invigoration to our minds. "Nothing can work me damage, except myself. The harm that I sustain I carry about in me; and never am a real sufferer but by my own fault."

And so the last truth which emerges from this story is that *character is fate*, to quote a well-known aphorism of Novalis. There is nothing fortuitous in such battles as this which Joseph fought; they are determined solely by character. What *are* we?

What equipment do we bring to the struggle? We may not be tempted precisely as Joseph was, but no man passes through life without his terrible hours of testing and temptation. And again I remind you that such hours come suddenly. We have no time to debate *then*, how we shall meet them; they are upon us before we know it. If the secrets of all hearts in this congregation were revealed; if we dared to speak of the things which we ourselves have known; how many of us could bear witness to these sudden temptations which break on the soul like the black squall upon a summer sea; and how many of us would shudder at the thought of how nearly we made shipwreck of life? Brethren, what saved us then, and what alone had power to save us? Simply this; the power of principle. It may be that we had absolutely nothing else on which we could rely. Perhaps the great temptation overtook us in a time when the intellectual difficulties of religion had proved too great for us, and all the old theologies in which we had been bred, had melted away. But we had something left — a stubborn conviction that nothing could make wickedness other than wicked, that God remained as the real witness and judge of our life, demanding truth in the inward parts, and we could say as F. W. Robertson said, "After finding littleness where I expected nobleness, and impurity where I thought there was spotlessness, again and again I despaired of the reality of goodness. But in all that struggle the bewilderment never told upon my conduct. Moral goodness and moral beauty are realities — they are no dream; and they are not mere utilitarian conveniences." And to say that is a great thing; yet a thing we all may say. It is a weapon which is invincible, a spell before which the most alluring vision of evil melts away. Brother, cleave to that; be sure that whatever changes, right and wrong change not; that though creeds may take a thousand forms, these have but one; and in your darkest, weakest, most tragic hour, learn to look up and say: —

> So near is glory to the dust,
> So nigh is God to man,
> When duty whispers low — Thou must,
> The youth replies — I can.

How can I do this great wickedness, and sin against God?

CHAMBERS OF IMAGERY

XIV

CHAMBERS OF IMAGERY

"What the ancients of the house of Israel do in the dark, everyone in the chambers of his imagery."—Ezekiel viii. 12.

THE chambers of imagery—a striking, suggestive phrase. It refers primarily to the practise of idolatry among the Israelites.

There were painted chambers, on whose walls all kinds of creatures associated with idolatry were depicted—

The shape of beasts and creeping things,
The body that availeth not.

There were pictures, too, of pagan deities, and all the voluptuous life of paganism—

Shapes on either wall,
Sea-coloured from some rare blue shell
At many a Tyrian interval,
Horsemen on horses, girdled well,
Delicate and desirable.

And in these secret chambers of imagery the heart of even the ancients of Israel grew corrupt. The Mosaic law practically forbade art, when it forbade the likeness being made of any living creature; and the Mosaic law still maintains this restriction, so that art among the Mohammedan races is confined to graceful intricate lines and arabesques; geometrical designs, but never the human form. It is hard for us to understand this restriction, but it is explained by the nature of the Oriental mind. Voluptuousness is one of the distinct characteristics of the Oriental, and among such races art soon becomes the servant of voluptuousness. The chamber of imagery was the picture gallery of a prostituted art; and from these chambers streamed forth the corruption of the nation.

These ancient idolatries have long since passed away, and the ancients of Israel no longer worship toward the East, uttering the name of Baal; and the women of Israel no longer weep for the Adonis of Greek Mythology, under another name, whose story was used to breed and inflame all the degenerate desires of the human heart. The ancient idolatries pass, but the spirit of idolatry is not so easily destroyed, and we still have our chambers of imagery. Our chamber of imagery is not built with hands, it is within ourselves. It is painted with no colours of human art; our thoughts are the artists, and our fancies are the things they paint. There is an inner life which we all live, so closely hidden from the world, that those who know us best, little suspect its nature and character. There is a secret chamber of the mind, the chamber of our imagination, where we live a life, to which the world holds no clue. Our real life is the life of our thought, our hope, our desire. And our thoughts are forever painting for us pictures which allure and delight us, which perhaps disgrace and debase us. In the mind of the saint hang sacred pictures, pictures of sacrifice, devotion, and heroic death; in the mind of the avaricious man, pictures of senseless opulence; in the mind of the profligate, pictures of extravagant and evil pleasures; in the mind of the ambitious man, pictures of immense triumph, world-wide coronation, endless power. From infancy to old age we dwell with these visions. Punished or neglected of the world, we retire into our chambers of imagery, and solace ourselves with the sweet delusion of our dreams. The dream-picture that thus glimmers perpetually on the walls of the imagination may be a seduction to our worse selves; it may be an impulse to our best selves; so that we may say,

> All my days I'll go the softlier, sadlier
> For that dream's sake.

But, whatever the nature of our dream-pictures, this is true of all of them, they rule us. Our imagination is the most potent element in our lives. It is in the chamber of imagery that our real life is lived, for what we desire, that we seek; what we covet, that we pursue; what we think, that we are.

The first thing I ask you to observe then, is that

we are the custodians of this inner and secret life, as well as of the outer and open life.

That we are the custodians of the outer life we all admit, and hence the great stress which the world lays on what is called behaviour. We know perfectly well that it is to our interest to exercise a sedulous care over the outward life. Hence, if we have any desire to succeed in life — and who has not this desire? — we cultivate the mind, we cultivate the grace of good manners, we cultivate the body that it may be efficient for its duties; so that externally, at least, we may become persons acceptable to our fellow-creatures. And there, you will observe, all that the world has to teach us about the custody of ourselves, stops. Among the great races of antiquity, bodily symmetry and beauty were the chief things; and to achieve physical perfection was to attain the ultimate reward of public praise. Among the ruling classes of the eighteenth century to be a man of honour was a sufficient passport to society, and honour in this case meant nothing more than a sufficient code of good behaviour. Among large classes of our fellow men to-day we find that to fulfil a certain social code is the one thing in demand; but all scrutiny of private morals is discouraged, and regarded as an unjust inquisition. Thus the inner life is generally ignored, and we are taught to ignore it. What did the Greek care for the private life of the athlete who won the applause of the populace by his physical beauty? What did the eighteenth century society care for the secret follies of its statesmen and its leaders, so long as they paid their betting debts, their debts of honour as they were called, and obeyed the lax conventions of superficial propriety? What does the world care still for the private life of the society queen, who charms men by her beauty, of the actress who pleases them by her art, or the man of genius who delights them with his gifts? And if you ask how it is that we come to reason thus, is it not because we have never grasped the truth that we are the custodians of an inner life, as well as an outward? We are responsible not only for our behaviour but for our souls. We have entrusted to us not only our body, not only the kind of man which is seen and judged by the physical eye, but an inner self, our thoughts, our emotions, our desires, our imagination. When we have regulated our conduct to society by the strictest code the world can give us, we have done but a very little thing; the great thing remaining to be done is to regulate our inner life before God, and to make that chamber of imagery where all our secret life is lived, a temple and a shrine.

Let me try to put the matter even more plainly. What is it I mean when I say that we have the custody over an inner life, as well as an outer? I mean that we have to determine what we think, as well as what we do, that we are responsible for the nature of our imaginations as well as of our acts.

That touches us more nearly, because very many of us assume that we have no control over our imaginative life. The pictures in the chamber of imagery paint themselves, we do not paint them. Visions of evil, infinitely seductive, float into the mind, we know not whence or how. We think that we have no responsibility for them, no more responsibility than the fertile earth has for the wind-blown thistle seed which may fall upon it, and because we think thus we make no effort to resist impure visions, or restrain evil ones. And so it happens that men whose outward lives are virtuous, often indulge themselves in evil visions, without so much as suspecting that they sin in doing it. Nay, more; they compensate themselves for the strictness of their outward virtue, by the riot of their secret thought. They turn to the chamber of imagery with an unconfessed delight, they abandon themselves to the seduction of thoughts they would not dare to utter, they act out in the theatre of the mind, dramas which would horrify them if they were transposed to the theatre of conduct. And if you question them on such things, they will say at once, "It surely matters little what I think, so long as my thought does not become an act. And under any circumstance I cannot control my thought, my fancy, and my imagination — these act for themselves independently of my will or my desire."

The answer to such arguments is threefold. First,

we have to remember that our imagination is extraordinarily sensitive, it is the most sensitive part of our nature, and therefore it is the point where sin attacks us first. There is a little instrument known to science as the radiometer. It is a tiny weathercock with a silver side to it; and so sensitive is it to light, that when the slightest beam of light impinges upon it, even though it is but the light of a candle many yards away, it begins slowly to revolve. In the same way the imagination is exquisitely sensitive, and that which stirs the imagination stirs the whole man. Set the imagination revolving, and its movement is at once communicated to the whole life.

Again, we have to recollect that debasement of any kind begins in debasement of imagination. We all remember how a great painter said that he never dared to look upon a bad picture, because for days afterwards it influenced him so powerfully that he could not paint well. He was deflected from true art by the mere memory of bad art, his draughtsmanship and colour suffered instantly, even by the recollection of an art which was inferior. Can it be a light thing, then, if we fill our chamber of imagery with bad pictures? Does not conduct instantly shape itself in correspondence with the imagination? Is not the thing we think in our private hours the compelling curve along which our public acts are bound to move?

And then we must remember, too, that the wisest

men have always recognised the danger of unrestrained imagination, and have claimed and exercised power to restrain it. If there be any virtue, *think* of these things, the things that are pure, lovely, and of good report, says St. Paul. You *can* think on them; it is a matter of will; and you can refuse to think on impure and unlovely things — that also is a matter of will. The door of the imagination does not stand wide open to all comers; and you, who would at once close the door of your home against the intrusion of the rabble, have you no power to close the door of the mind against the rabble thoughts that defile it? You have that power; you may be master of your thoughts if you will, even as you are master of your speech, and master of your habits; and against all the poor sophistry which assumes the inability of the imagination to defend itself, which claims that the pictures on the walls paint themselves, which disclaims responsibility for them, and treats them as of small account, stand those facts of life to which all wise men bear witness, that we can help what we think, and that it is of the highest moment that we should watch our thoughts, since what we think we are. "Let no man say when he is tempted, I am tempted of God; for God cannot be tempted with evil, neither tempteth He any man, but every man is tempted, when he is drawn away of his own lust and enticed." Consider that saying of St. James and then you will see that it is neither God nor Satan who paints the picture on the wall; we are the artists and the audience, we are the tempter and the tempted, we are the sinners and the victims.

Chambers of imagery. How ought we to think of our imaginations? Let us turn to Scripture for a moment that we may understand how we ought to think of our imaginations. There are many things in the Bible on which we may hold divergent views, but there is one thing on which we can scarcely disagree — the essential truth of the estimate of human nature which the Bible gives us. The Bible alone of all great books in the world does not flatter man. Some of you will perhaps recollect how Browning deals with this truth in one of his most striking poems. He pictures to us a woman who hid under the smile of a saint, a sordid vice which was not discovered till she was dead. And then he goes on to say that here is an illustration of all that Christianity has to say about original sin. It is the fashion, he says, of modern teachers to flatter men; to take rose-water views of life; to proclaim how radically good man is; but not so Christianity, she

> launched point-blank her dart,
> At the head of a lie; taught original sin,
> The corruption of man's heart.

And when the Bible speaks of man's heart it means his imagination. The accusation God makes against man is, that "every imagination of the thoughts of his heart is only evil continually." It is in the chamber of imagery that all the corruption of human life begins.

Take the decalogue. There are ten commandments, eight of which have to do with outward conduct. Then comes the tenth, the last, the consummating commandment, the top of this great staircase of morality, and what is the tenth commandment? *Thou shalt not covet* — something that grows in the mind and the imagination. You may remove at a stroke three commandments that precede it: they are unnecessary if the tenth be kept, for without the picture of things we covet which inflame the imagination, who would kill or steal or commit adultery? "Covetousness, which is idolatry," says the Apostle, and is not the definition accurate? And is it not in the chambers of imagery that we accustom ourselves to these visions which translate themselves on some apt opportunity into murder, theft, and adultery, into false witness which smooths the path of our ambition, into the dishonour shown to parents who are a hindrance to our pride, or the contempt of the Sabbath that we may squeeze a little more work or a little more pleasure out of our days: into that making of graven images, before which we bow down at last and worship, even as the ancients of Israel bowed down before the painted figures on the wall? *Thou shalt not covet* — it is the sum of all the commandments, and coveting is not an act; it is a temper, it is a process of the imagination, it is a thing so secret to ourselves that none but ourselves know that it exists.

Take, again, that most striking parable of Christ's, the Empty House, which is surely the House of the Mind and Imagination. Behold the house swept and garnished, for by a violent effort the man has stopped the riot of his thoughts, he has closed the drama, he has driven the actors out into the darkness. Here at least is the hint of man's power over his inner life, a hint that has been acted on by multitudes of men who have sought to scourge themselves into purity, to reduce the mind into emptiness rather than allow it licence, to break up the whole mechanism of life in a desperate effort to resist the temptations of life. But then follows something infinitely more subtle; Christ says you cannot keep the house of the Imagination empty. It is not enough to draw the disfiguring brush over the painted wall; the eye resents mere blankness. There are other pictures that must be painted there, there is a noble drama that must be enacted if you would forget the ignoble, for evil is only overcome with good. This is what the man of the parable forgets, and so the expelled actors, finding the house empty, come back, re-inforced and clamorous by exile, and the last state of that man is worse than the first. Look at that parable, and do you not at once see that it is a mental state which it describes?

Do you not feel that Christ means it to be a solemn lesson on the use and perversion of the imagination in mankind?

Or turn once more to that fearful picture, not less fearful than true, of the absolute unspeakable corruption of pagan life which Paul gives us in his Epistle to the Romans, and then take note of what he describes to be the root of this corruption. "They became vain in their imaginations, and their foolish hearts were darkened." Those who have written of those abominations of pagan life which find a record in such frescoes as one may still see at Pompeii, have usually spoken as if these things were the fruit of moral decay; Paul would have called them not the fruit, but the seed, not the effect, but the cause. The corruption of imagination preceded the corruption of life, and art has recorded that corrupt imagination for us. And so it has always been; so it will ever be; it is that which proceedeth out of a man's heart that defileth him. And hence all redemption begins with the redemption of thought; all purification with purity of mind, and it is in the chamber of imagery that those forces are begotten that redeem the soul, even as it is there also that the forces are begotten which destroy it.

And now let me put to you this one question: What is it that goes on in your Chamber of Imagery? I need not point out the bearing of all that I have said on a young man's life, because we know well, that if ever the imagination is strong in us, it is in the days of youth. In that painted chamber of your mind, in that dim-lit theatre of your thought, the acts of all your future life rehearse themselves. Have you taken any serious notice of what goes on within you? Have you treated this incessant drama of your fancy merely as a pastime? Have you taken any pains to direct or curb this drama, to feed the mind with right thoughts, to supply this restless artist, which we call the Imagination, with right materials and right models, so that the picture on the wall shall be one you will not be ashamed for all the world to see, in the day when the secrets of all hearts are revealed?

Do you, for instance, exercise any circumspection in your talk? There is a kind of talk, all too common among youths, which poisons the imagination; do you indulge yourself in this talk? Or do you take any serious care in the selection of the books you read? There are books also which defile the mind, and which may fill it with ineffaceable pictures which are so many incentives to evil; do you read them, not in the dispassionate way a critic might read them, but by preference and with greediness? And there are forms of art, also, which are a prostitution of art, even as in the ancient days of paganism; and do you seek these, passing by all that is great and noble, all that is uplifting, that the lust of the eye may satiate itself upon things unworthy and even base? These are plain questions; believe me they go to the very heart of life. Yet we are for the most part careless of them; and so long as our life is decent we trouble ourselves little or not at all over the nature of our thoughts, forgetting this most solemn truth that our thoughts are but our acts rehearsed.

The chamber of imagery; could I indeed look into it, I should know all that there is to be known about you. We say sometimes that we may judge a man by his books, or by the company he keeps; we may judge him yet more accurately by the chamber of imagery in which he loves to dwell. When I saw the newly-opened apartments of the Borgias in the Vatican at Rome, I seemed to see in those walls covered with gay and brilliant and voluptuous frescoes, all the history of the Borgias. When I stood, later, in the bare and quiet cell of Savonarola in Florence, I also read the secret of the man. In the one the voluptuous, in the other the austere; in the one the vain shows of life, in the other the serenity of eternity; the one a banqueting house, the other a shrine. Each has left his record on the wall, and he who knows least of history feels the difference. He knows that Christ never trod within that splendid chamber of the profligate Pope, but that often Christ stood in that narrow cell, where Savonarola wept, and prayed, and toiled for the redemption of the city he loved so well.

And so, I ask you, what are the pictures on the walls, what is the chamber of your imagery — a place of infamy or a shrine?

I would plead with you for the religious culture of the imagination. I would implore you to treat your imagination seriously and reverently. I would ask you to notice in literature, if nowhere else, and there chiefly because the example is most readily perceived, the evil wrought by impure imagination, and the good wrought by the sanctified imagination, that you may learn how large a part imagination plays in influencing character. And then, I would ask you to enter your chamber of imagery, and ascertain what are the pictures on the walls. It may be that with some of you they are corrupt; with others they are merely vain and foolish pictures, which are incapable of inspiring any lofty deed or noble thought. O, that I could replace them with other pictures! O, that it were in my power to fill your imagination with those immortal pictures from which the lives of men have received their noblest impulse and direction, these many centuries! For I would fain paint there a picture of the joyous innocence of Christ, that looking on it you might know how blessed is the man who is pure in heart. I would paint the picture of Jesus in His helpfulness towards mankind; with the little children in His arms, and the Magdalen at His feet, that you might know how happy is the life that is spent in doing good. And I would paint Him as He dies, young, ardent, beloved, yet willing to be sacrificed, that you might know what Divine triumph there is in the life that gives itself for others. And then over all these pictures I would paint a scroll, on which these words should shine in starry clearness, "Behold, I have given you an example; let the mind that was in Christ Jesus be in you." These are pictures which never fade, and in them the best life of the world has been nourished for nearly two thousand years. These are the pictures that make the chamber of imagery a temple and a shrine; and from such a shrine there flows not the influence that corrupts but redeems, there issues forth the life that is wise and lofty, pure and noble, and which has that divinest of all beauties, the beauty of Holiness.

THE REPROACH OF THE FLOWER

XV

THE REPROACH OF THE FLOWER

A FLOWER SERMON

"And is not the life more than meat?"—St. Matt. vi. 25.

"And ye have therefore received Jesus Christ, the Lord, so walk ye in Him, rooted and built up in Him."—Col. ii. 6, 7.

WHAT is the clearest thought, the most vivid impression that comes to us when we gather in such a service as this? Here there are around me the flowers of the earth, these delicate, fragile purities and fragrances of the fields and gardens, each fashioned in exquisite art, each contributing elements of delight to the senses, each, as it were, a poem in colour, a symphony in grace. Is not the clearest impression this, that here we have the manifestations of a life, a life apparently quite different in essence and quality from life as it exists among men? Man's life is often a thing of sorrow and of labour; it is difficult, it is perplexed, it is threatened; but here is a kind of life that seems to be simple and instinctive. Man, with infinite toil, builds up for himself a beautiful edifice of life: the flower, in silence and in the concord of all its parts and qualities, comes easily to its perfection. "The lily toils not nor spins," says Jesus; yet it is arrayed in a glory which Solomon, in all his splendour and with all his seeking, never knew. A life, that is what we are confronted with, and a life different from our own. Side by side with our vexed human life, there is going on at this moment, throughout the wide world, a sweeter and a more gracious kind of life, of which we rarely think. Men may be counted, but who shall take a census of the flowers? Year by year the innumerable army of the flowers, beneath the banner of the sunlight, comes marching up over field and pasture, to possess the earth; a living army, called forth by the breath of the Almighty. Think of that vast invasion, picture to yourself the delicate strength of this living host, and then you will come to some sense of the Divine mystery of life itself; and that is what Jesus would have you think when He turns from the contemplation of the flowers of the field, and says to this weary, anxious congregation gathered at His feet, "Is not the life, that life you are looking at, more than meat?"

Read with care this familiar and gracious passage of the Sermon on the Mount, and I think you will see at once that this is Christ's thought, and you will see how He applies it. Christ sees the life of man, and what impresses Him most in the life of man, is its distraction, its disquietude, its misguidance. Christ sees the life of nature, and what impresses Him most in the life of nature, is its serenity, its efficiency, the sureness of its development. The flower has, or seems to have, the happiness that man has not; it fulfils its true nature, which man seldom does. The lilies of the field are man's reproach. For, while man tramples over the whole earth with the lust of wealth or the lust of war in his heart, spoiling all he touches and spoiling himself in the process, the flower simply grows in obedience to Divine laws, written in its own nature. And the beauty of God rests upon the flowers of the field, while ugliness and distortion mark the path of man. What then is wrong with man? Who is at fault that man, with all his infinite variety of powers, should stand ashamed before the humblest flower? The fault lies in man, and with man, because he has forgotten that the life is more than meat, he is more concerned over externals than internals, he acts as if his creed were that it is more important to get a living than to live, he seeks not to *be* something, but to *get* something. And it is from that cardinal error that Christ would redeem us by the healing spectacle of Nature. Nature works with but one object — the perfection of all her creatures. Her great concern is with the life, the adequate development of all the possibilities of life in each. Let man learn this lesson for himself, and then he will be on the way to be perfect, " even as the Father in Heaven is perfect." Let him root and ground himself in the thoughts of Jesus, and the world will again become the paradise and the very garden of God. But until man does this the flower will be his reproach; he will stand ashamed before it, because the flower is for him the type of a perfect life which he, with all his seeking, does not find.

The reproach of the flower — that then seems to me to be Christ's suggestion to us. Christ comes to us with the lilies of the field in His hand, and says, "Look at these, and then look upon your own soiled imperfect life; come into the green places of the earth and rest with Me awhile that ye may learn of Me whom poets and prophets call the Lily of the Valley, the Rose of Sharon." There is a kind of life of which the flower is the living parable, asking from the world only the simplest things, becoming beautiful not for the sake of praise but for the satisfaction of laws written in its own nature, content to add a little brightness to the world and to cheer the hearts of men. The life of the flower — look at it and, when you look, ask whether the flower is not a reproach to you.

The reproach of the flower. First of all, we may say that the reproach of the flower is *the reproach of simplicity.* Why does Christ bid us look upon the flowers? Have they any spiritual lessons to impart? Yes, they have the great lesson, and surely it is a spiritual lesson, of simplicity. Who is there of us who has not at some time or other felt this revelation of the beautiful simplicity that is in nature, when in summer days we have turned away from the city for a little time, and have sought the ancient haunts of peace where Nature is? Do you recall your reflections? If you recall them, did they not run somewhat in this channel? Did you not find yourself thinking in your own mind, "How poor and vain and vexed and trivial does that life seem that I I have been living, compared with this life where I know 'the silence that is in the starry sky, the sleep that is among the lonely hills?' How keenly do I feel that in all this stress and rush of city life, I may have followed but a vain dream, and disquieted myself in vain. Here is the old sweet life of Nature going on in such perfect quietness, and I am so full of disquietude and of anxiety." And then there came to you the thought that in the midst of this busy life of yours, perhaps you had really not lived at all. You had denied yourself "leisure to grow wise and shelter to grow ripe." The bank account had grown, it may be, but somehow you felt the soul had not thrived, and there came to you the revelation of simplicity; there came to you the thought that possibly, after all, your character would have been serener, your heart would have known more of the living pulse of joy, if you had lived a simple and a quiet life close to the heart of Nature. That was when the flower reproached you, that was when you felt the reproach of the flower, and as you passed through the fields every daisy seemed to turn its eye up to you and rebuke you with the distraction, the lack of simplicity, the lack of content that was in your life.

"The life is more than meat," says Christ. What life? The word which Christ uses means "soul," for you recollect that upon another occasion Christ uses the same phrase when He says, "What shall it profit a man if he gain the whole world and lose his own life, or his own soul?" Why are you not able to live a simple life? Let me say in parenthesis, by the phrase "simple life" I do not mean a life necessarily lived in the hamlet, or on the hill side, or in the lonely valley. Simple lives may be lived anywhere. But why is it we cannot live simple lives? It is because we do not believe in the soul enough. You do not feel God's life within you. If you did, you would care for no other life. Christ saw in His day a vast society, a vast civilisation, devoting all its energies to the creation of pleasures for the body, and He gave the true reason for it all. He said, in effect, that the Gentile nations had lost faith in the soul, and He stated plainly that material luxury, the growth of luxury, is the sole beatitude of Paganism. Where there is no genuine faith in the soul, no sense of God's life in us, then there is bound to follow the materialisation of society. But a revived faith in the soul always brings with it simplification of life. We are all ready to discuss the simple life to-day because we are all of us only too conscious of many elements of weariness in the complicated life we live, but let us be sure of this, it is nothing but a spiritual revival that will make the simple life possible to us. We must find anew the God of the lilies before we are able to live in the quiet places where the lilies grow. And, if you think for a moment what the past history of our race has to teach, you will see how true that reflection is, for you will see that simplification of life has always followed the new birth of spirituality. The moment Buddha grasps the great truth that he is an emanation from God, that God is all, and in all, he can leave the palace and be a cheerful beggar by the wayside. The material has perished because the spiritual is born. In the same way St. Paul says that he knows "how to be abased and how to abound." Fulness and poverty are alike nothing to him, because his soul is lost in God. And it was so with Wordsworth. From the moment when the great thought of the mysticism of Nature possessed him, he preferred poverty with the vision of Nature to wealth without it. These men are different, their ideals, their methods and speech are different, but they are united in a real unity of experience. From the hour when the highest things possess them the spell of the lower things is broken. And as it was with these men so it has always been throughout the long history of the ages. It was so with the early Christians; the birth of the soul in them, delivered them from the yoke of materialism and the care for material luxury. It was so with the Puritans; living ever as in their Taskmaster's eye, they were indifferent to the praises of the world. And it must be so with us if ever we are to get that note of simplification struck again. But the simplification of society, lives of higher thinking, lives of plainer living, lives of purer feeling, will have to come through the rebirth of spiritual instinct and spiritual desires.

My brethren, are we rooted and grounded then in the simplicity of Christ? We can only become so by being rooted in the spirituality of Christ. We look back to that sacred idyll of Christ's Galilean ministry, and we think, possibly, how glorious and sweet it would have been to have walked with Him there by the lake's side and in the field of the lilies, listening to His talk, Who spake as never man spake of the things of Nature; but have you not noticed that those who were His companions in these scenes were all of them quite unworldly people; they were people who had given up all because they thought it worth while to give up all for the sake of the Divine comradeship? And it is so still. Simplification of life is found in increased spirituality of thought. The root of Christ's life was in God, and, if we are rooted in Christ as Christ was rooted in God, then there may come to us the possibility of that quiet, simple, contented life that Jesus Himself lived in the fields of Galilee.

The reproach of the flower — it is again the re-

proach of faithfulness. "Faithfulness," we say: "pray what has faithfulness to do with the flower of the field?" Christ evidently thought it had something to do with it, for you will notice that He closes this talk about the flowers of the field with the sad apostrophe, "O ye of little faith!" Suppose for a moment one could attribute consciousness to these flowers, and that we could question them about the nature of their life, what sort of answer would they give? Might not the flower be imagined as replying to us thus: "I am but a tiny thing under the wide firmament with its great sun and its mystery of glittering stars, yet I know that I am not forgotten. Dews and sunbeams and rain and wind all come to me, each in its appointed season. Little as I am, I am God's partner in weaving the pageantry of summer. I do my little part in a humble place but I know that God has dealings with me. There is a kind of faith in me, faith that God will care for me, faith that God cares for my beauty and my perfection, and so I am faithfully doing the exact thing God has given me to do, and waiting that God may do for me the thing I cannot do for myself." That is the confession of the flower. Is it our confession? How rare is such a confession on human lips! How few of us do really feel God's partnership in our little life! Throughout all Nature there lies this deep abiding law of faithfulness, the quiet fulfilment of the Divine plan, the meek acquiescence in the Divine will, the whole creation resting on its God and waiting patiently for Him. But in man there is little of this faithfulness. And so the flower reproaches us. And He Who speaks of flowers, and Whose life was one beautiful unfolding of meekness and faith, reproaches us in saying: "If God so clothe the grass of the field which to-day is and to-morrow is cast into the oven, shall He not much more clothe you, O ye of little faith!" Rooted in Christ — are we rooted in the steadfast faith and patience of Christ? For among all those great qualities which the life of Christ reveals to men, first of all stands His faithfulness. He never once murmured at His lot, even when it was hardest; He never scorned the place appointed for Him, even when it was lowliest. Most wonderful of all things in that wondrous life is the composure of Christ's mind, His serene trust in God. He felt the partnership with God in His life, with a completeness that no other ever realised. "I and the Father are One." Nothing could separate Him from God, not even the great dereliction of the Cross. And to be rooted in Christ is to have the same spirit of entire faithfulness, producing entire humility and composure and the peaceful unfolding of the soul into a beauty which is for God's eye alone, as it is wrought alone by the grace and the spirit of God.

The reproach of the flower — it is, once more, *the*

reproach of beauty. If there is one thing in which all agree when we gaze at flowers, it is this — we feel the charm of their beauty. But, if we come to analyse beauty, what is beauty but another word for completeness? Why is the flower beautiful? Because it is complete. You could not better it, with all your thinking, though you thought for a lifetime; you could not add to the lily of the field, or even to the daisy, a single element that would be an added grace. It is complete. A friend of mine last week was good enough to send me some exquisite specimens of the bee-orchid with their marvellous mimicry of life, and as I looked upon that mimicry of life I felt the wonder of it, I felt that these flowers were flower-miracles; but yesterday I cut a common garden rose — and but a poor one at that — and looked into its beautiful convolutions for a moment before the petals fell, and the thought came to me that after all that was quite as marvellous as the bee-orchid, and quite as beautiful. For wherever there is completeness there is beauty. The design of God is so uniformly beautiful that we have only to obey the design to attain beauty, and it is only when we disregard the design of God that we arrive at ugliness. Show me completeness anywhere, in the daisy, in the rose, in the child, in the human mind, in the development of a human life, and you show me beauty. And there is no beauty where there is not completeness. But of all beautiful things in this world, a complete human life is the most beautiful. I mentioned in a recent address an article which had struck me in one of the art magazines, an article describing Claydon House in Buckinghamshire. The house is one of the houses beautiful of England. Pages were taken up with descriptions of its carvings, its pictures, its staircases, the marvels of its wrought iron and exquisite marqueterie, and so forth; and then at the very end of the article it was mentioned that there was a little plain room upstairs that had no art adornment whatever, but it was in that room Florence Nightingale dwelt. And on the walls were no historic pictures, but only crude scenes in the Crimean War. Only that. Ah! but I felt that that room was the true shrine of the whole place. There a soul had lived, there a spiritual life had gone on, and that was the glory of the house. It gave a beauty to it. You can get no beauty in human life except through the beautiful soul. Houses are poor things until love comes into them and makes them homes, and the house of life is a poor thing until the spirit of God takes possession of the inner shrine and makes the life complete. Would you live a beautiful life? Let it be a complete life, and what this completion is the great Apostle tells you — Rooted in Christ, grounded in Christ, established in Christ — and here is the final phrase, "*complete in Him.*" That life alone I count a beautiful life which is a complete life, and for the true completion of our life we must be rooted in Christ, and grow in His grace, that we may attain to His image.

The reproach of beauty. As our eyes rest on these exquisite and perfected works of Nature's art, do we feel the reproach of beauty, do we feel how unbeautiful our lives often are, how little of grace and perfume there is in them, how thwarted and impoverished and deflected from God's design they are? Why? The reason with many of us — and I speak now to those who call themselves Christians — the reason is that we are rooted *upon* Christ, rather than rooted *in* Christ; we are parasites. The ivy clings to the oak, but it is easily separable from it, because it has no part in the root and in the life of the oak; so some of us are clinging to the surfaces of Christianity, to its outward forms and functions, but our root has never yet struck deep into the life of Christ. The roots of your life, the fibres in which the vital sap runs, what of these? You and I can answer that question best for ourselves. For some of us, it may be, that the real root of our life is in pride and vanity; for others it is in worldliness and pleasure; for others it is in secret sins and in the corrupt and evil will. And there can be no beauty in such a life, there will blossom no perfect flower from such a root. Look to the roots of your life then, for that is the final message of the flowers. All that is of beauty in the flowers has its source is something that is out of sight. So the beautiful life is a life whose root is hid with Christ in God. Of all the world's great needs to-day, there is no need so great as a more pure and perfect life among Christians. It is the poor and dwarfed blossom of moral beauty that we find in the lives that are called Christian that is the great hindrance to Christianity. Remember, creeds and professions have very little weight with men now-a-days — less than they ever had. It is lives that count, and to-day, as in the early days of Christianity, it is the spectacle of lives, manifestly beautiful in ideals and conduct, in spirit and temper, that set men thinking, and presently set them seeking for the secret of Jesus. How are we to live such lives? Only by being rooted in Christ, rooted in His faith, rooted in His character, His thoughts, His deeds, His spirit and temper. He calls us, He entreats us to share His most secret life, telling us that He is the Vine and we are the branches. And so let us join in prayer to the Vine of God, that He may take our lives into His own, we rooted in Him and He in us for evermore.

Deep strike Thy root, O Heavenly Vine,
  Within our earthly sod,
Most beautiful, yet most divine,
  The Flower of man and God.

Rooted, grounded, stablished, complete in Christ — that is the life beautiful that we each may live, and this is also " life eternal to know the only true God and Jesus Christ whom He hath sent."

THE END